PRAISE FOR
CALLED TO GREATNESS

"This book is a must-read for anyone looking to achieve their full potential. Auerbach's insights into the science of peak performance are both illuminating and actionable. With his guidance, you'll learn how to develop the mental skills and habits you need to succeed in any area of life."

—**Steve Magness,** author of *Win the Inside Game: How to Move from Surviving to Thriving, and Free Yourself Up to Perform* and *Do Hard Things: Why We Get Resilience Wrong and the Surprising Science of Real Toughness*

"Alex Auerbach is one of the most thoughtful sport and performance psychologists there is. *Called to Greatness* is chock-full of concepts, insights, and practical applications to help you get the best out of yourself, both in day-to-day life and when you are called to meet the moment in peak occasions."

—**Brad Stulberg,** bestselling author of *The Practice of Groundedness: A Transformative Path to Success That Feeds—Not Crushes—Your Soul* and *Master of Change: How to Excel When Everything Is Changing—Including You*

"Dr. Alex Auerbach's *Called to Greatness* is a clear guide for high performers looking to unlock their full potential. Dr. Auerbach provides scientific insights and hard-earned practical wisdom to provide a road map for achieving peak performance—consistently. His experience with elite performers is the foundation for the tools he shares with readers to help them to cultivate mental strength, resilience, and sustained excellence. This is a must-read for those seeking to elevate their lives."

—**Greg Wells, Ph.D.,** author of *The Ripple Effect: Sleep Better, Eat Better, Move Better, Think Better* and senior scientist at the Hospital for Sick Children in Toronto, Canada

"Peak performance isn't about luck—it's about preparation. Dr. Auerbach's work has been powerful in my own leadership."

—**Morra Aarons-Mele,** host of *The Anxious Achiever* podcast and author of *The Anxious Achiever: Turn Your Biggest Fears into Your Leadership Superpower*

"With *Called to Greatness*, you'll learn how to strengthen your mindset, boost your resilience, and achieve the kind of success that lasts."

—**Erik Korem, Ph.D.**, sports scientist and founder/CEO of AIM7

"*Called to Greatness* is a powerful guide for anyone who believes in the transformative power of fitness and mental performance to elevate our lives. What makes it stand out is its holistic approach to peak performance. Auerbach doesn't just tell us to 'push harder'—he emphasizes self-care, recovery, and mental resilience as essential components of long-term success. He highlights how well-being is crucial to achieving and sustaining high-level performance, making this an invaluable playbook for those who understand that fitness is as much about mental and emotional strength as it is physical."

—**Krista Stryker,** fitness expert, author of *The 12-Minute Athlete: Get Fitter, Faster, and Stronger Using HIIT and Your Bodyweight,* chief performance coach at the Center for Human Potential, and creator of the *On Fire* newsletter

"Alex Auerbach has spent his career coaching some of the greatest athletes and most successful executives on the planet. Now, in *Called to Greatness*, his first book, he shares what he's learned for the world to benefit from. Lucid, comprehensive, and actionable, *Called to Greatness* is filled with lessons that won't just improve your performance—they'll improve your life."

—**Ethan Kross,** international bestselling author of *Chatter: The Voice in Our Head, Why It Matters, and How to Harness It* and *Shift: Managing Your Emotions—So They Don't Manage You*

"I vividly remember Alex telling me the story of how he got into psychology, and how it felt like a calling. He has become my go-to partner for anything to do with peak performance, and this book gives you a glimpse into why. Alex not only has an encyclopedic knowledge of studies and models that can help, he has opinions and experiences to make them contextual and applicable. Sport psychology was Alex's call to greatness, and this book is yours."

—**Cody Royle,** coach of head coaches, author and keynote speaker

CALLED TO GREATNESS

Alex Auerbach

CALLED TO GREATNESS

Your personal **playbook** for the pursuit of **excellence**

Copyright © 2025 by Alex Auerbach

All rights reserved. No part of this publication may be reproduced, distributed, or transmitted in any form or by any means, including photocopying, recording, or other electronic or mechanical methods, without the prior written permission of the publisher, except as permitted by U.S. copyright law. For permission requests, contact Life to Paper Publishing at info@lifetopaper.com.

The information provided in this book is for educational purposes only and is not intended as a substitute for consultation with a licensed practitioner. The use of this book implies your acceptance of this disclaimer.

First Edition 2025

Paperback ISBN: 978-1-990700-63-7
eBook ISBN: 978-1-990700-64-4

Library of Congress Control Number: 2024916070

Interior design by Mary Beth MacLean
Cover design by Elbert D. Foster

Printed in the U.S.A.

1 2 3 4 5 6 7 8 9 10

Life to Paper Publishing Inc.
Toronto | Miami
www.lifetopaper.com

*This book is dedicated to my wife, Kirstie,
and our daughters Zosia and Wiley.*

Each of you, in your own way, has made it feel like it was possible to finish this. This book wouldn't exist without you.

I love you.

CONTENTS

Introduction: We Are All Called to Greatness .... *xi*

Part 1: The Qualities of Typical Performance

Introduction 2
Quality #1: Capacity 3
Quality #2: Mental Strength 27
Quality #3: Endurance 53
Quality #4: Flexibility 79
Quality #5: Self-Regulation 97

Part 2: The Principles of Peak Performance

Introduction 112
Principle #1: Preparation 115
Principle #2: Immersion 143
Principle #3: Adaptation 165
Principle #4: Energy Optimization 185
Principle #5: Resilience 207

Conclusion: We Are All Called to Greatness 227
Acknowledgments 229
Index 231
About the Author 235

INTRODUCTION:
WE ARE ALL CALLED TO GREATNESS

Welcome to your high-performance handbook. This book is my endeavor to synthesize two parts of the human experience that have both fascinated me and informed my performance coaching philosophy: what allows humans to perform at their best when it matters most, and what enables humans to reach their full potential.

For the last fifteen years, I've spent my career (in various capacities) exploring what enables high performers to deliver *consistent* results and make meaningful progress toward achieving their full potential. I've seen the synergistic benefits that can result from having a focus on maximizing what's possible. Those benefits play out in critical moments—the game-winning shot, the pitch to investors, the challenging conversations with children—and over a lifetime in terms of well-being and living a meaningful life.

During this fifteen-year stretch, I've had the opportunity to coach college football, work in the NBA and NFL, provide coaching services to Fortune 500 companies, and attend live demolition training at one of the premier military bases in the United States. I've spent time training US Parajumpers how to remain calm and decisive while defusing bombs, coached professional athletes and Olympians to have the performance of a lifetime, and helped entrepreneurs build unicorns. Along the way, I completed my Ph.D. in psychology, a field with a focus on human strengths and questions like "What makes for a good life?"

What I've come to believe is that to achieve peak performance is to follow a set of principles that maximize the odds of delivering under pressure. All performances are odds-based events. We can make mistakes and still win, and do everything right and still fall short. The principles introduced here serve as a formula we can use to tilt the odds in our favor.

As impressive as these performances can be, the best performers I have worked with do something else that's significant. They don't just focus on the biggest moments. They focus on being their best time and again, until they stop being the best and become, to borrow a phrase from Naval Ravikant, "the only."

This focus defines a life guided by fulfilling potential. This formula is not solely the domain of athletes; it's a motivational tool to lead a better life.

To consistently perform at your peak, you have to start with a set of practices that raises your overall well-being and puts you in a position to deliver under pressure. With that strong foundation in place, you're in a much better position to pursue excellence and work at becoming the best version of yourself.

* * *

As a performance psychologist, I'm constantly thinking about two types of performance. The first type, ***typical performance***, is how you perform in your day-to-day. It's the way you deliver on the things you're consistently asked to do. If you're a parent, your typical performance is how you show up every day when you raise your kid. If you're a CEO, your typical performance is how you lead on an average Wednesday. If you're an athlete, your typical performance is how you perform during the regular season. The five skills (what I call qualities) discussed in part one—capacity, mental strength, endurance, flexibility, and self-regulation—are all about creating a strong foundation to consistently raise our typical level of performance.

In part one, you'll uncover ways you can stretch your capabilities, how psychological flexibility can promote your long-term health, and the single skill that separates the best athletes and performers in the world from their slightly less skilled counterparts. You'll discover how to raise your game so your baseline becomes better and better.

In part two, you'll be introduced to the second type of performance—*peak performance*. This is the performance we typically see when we watch our favorite players in action, or hear or read about the heroic achievements of medical professionals and volunteers in the line of fire, be it war or a pandemic. It's performance under the highest pressure and brightest lights, and it is here we reach the next level and establish a new personal best. The principles of peak performance are preparation, immersion, adaptability, energy optimization, and resilience.

I will introduce you to the science-backed performance principles I use to coach. We'll cover how to get ready to perform, how to optimize your energy and focus, and how to respond resiliently to adverse conditions and setbacks. You'll meet some of the world's best performers and be shown how they use these principles to deliver optimum results. We'll also uncover performance pitfalls and what you can do to ensure you're in the right frame of mind to perform when the pressure is on. This is what psychologists call "maximal performance": how you deliver under the biggest circumstances.

Because we're not seeking a particular core set of skills to the exclusion of everything else, we're free to shift our focus to what's most important: what works. Elite performers drop the notion of "right" and "wrong," and look for what works for them. You should look for what works for you too by selecting the skills I will introduce based on your performance needs. The art of performance psychology lies in applying these skills in a way that is unique to the performance at hand.

I'm confident that the skills I'll ask you to try will help you deliver more consistent, higher-level performances. I'm also confident that this book can help you live a richer, more meaningful and engaging life. The information is based on decades of research and my experience working with high performers. But don't just believe me—get started and see the results for yourself.

PART 1:

THE QUALITIES OF TYPICAL PERFORMANCE

INTRODUCTION

As you will discover in reading and applying the concepts and activities in this book, peak performance is holistic. Whether you're a parent, leader, salesperson, or CEO, the path to being your best when it matters most starts at the same place. You need to build a strong foundation of well-being. You simply can't perform at your best if you're not well, nor can you feel fulfilled.

What good is it to win a gold medal, and while walking off the podium, wish you were someone else or somewhere else? While it's tough to imagine an athlete who has proved they are the best in the world having such negative thoughts and doubting their very being, high performers can and do feel lost as soon as they reach the peak. They wonder if they can do it again, if the hard work and effort were worth it, if they want to keep going. They fail to fall in love with the process or develop themselves outside of sports. So they keep moving the goal posts farther and farther out, hoping that achieving more will lead to more fulfilment.

But does achieving more actually lead to fulfilment?

We need to make the most of our *life* holistically, not just our performances. In part one of this book, I'll introduce you to a set of psychological skills that will help you flourish. These competencies form the building blocks of wellness. You'll discover what you can do to stretch your capacity, build mental strength, and master some psychological tools to get past roadblocks and break through to the next level of performance.

To begin that journey, we start with building *capacity*.

QUALITY #1:

Capacity

If I have the belief that I can do it, I shall surely acquire the capacity to do it, even if I may not have it at the beginning.

– *Mahatma Gandhi*

Elite performance requires complete wellness. You can't perform if you're not well. In sports, we tend to take much better care of the physical health of our athletes and overlook what it means to be mentally well. Western culture has over-indexed on an attitude of toughness. Unfortunately, that attitude leads people to push away or hide how they really feel. We can see a physical injury, but it's harder to detect something going on inside someone. On top of that, most of us aren't provided with the education or training that can help us sustain our well-being and pursue excellence over the long term.

The good news is that pro sports is going through a cultural shift that will hopefully lead the way for reforming the rest of our achievement-oriented culture. Professional sports organizations are starting to realize that for players to perform well, they must *feel* well. Much like running on a bad knee or ankle, the joint might take the strain for a while, but over time if not rested will break down and require a respite to heal. Human beings may be able to cope with poor mental health for a little while, but if prolonged can become debilitative. Rest and recovery will be required.

We're starting to see this approach made more public too. Athletes are starting to sit out when they don't feel mentally ready; they are aware of the risks of trying to power through. Simone Biles, Michael Phelps, Kevin Love, and Naomi Osaka (among others) have made it clear that their mental health is their priority. Their message to fans is clear: I can't give you my best right now, and I need to rebuild before I return.

At the same time, some of the best athletes have quietly been prioritizing their well-being all along. The winningest Formula 1 racer of all-time, Lewis Hamilton, puts feeling well at the heart of his training. "The better you feel, the better you are at doing your job," he says. Isn't this true for all of us? Can't we do more and perform better when we are well?

In this chapter, we'll unpack how to build your capacity so that you have what you need in the gas tank to succeed time and again. You'll learn how to be well. You'll come to know yourself better and to know what you need to be at your best. Being able to deliver time and again, in different circumstances is the hallmark of capacity and excellence. This is the foundation for getting there.

WHAT IS ADAPTIVE CAPACITY?

Reaching our full potential in life is about progressively getting better. As trite as that sounds, there's a scientific principle that underlies our ability to take on higher, harder challenges. That principle is adaptive capacity. You can think of adaptive capacity like building a muscle. You exercise a muscle, then rest, and as you repeat the process it grows stronger. The next time you get to the gym or hit the track, you can lift a little bit more or run a little bit faster. Your adaptive capacity has increased, and you're improving.

The same thing is true with our mental muscles. Just like physical conditioning, mental conditioning requires us to take on challenges, recover and tackle another challenge. By taking on challenges and giving yourself time to recover, you'll be able to take on higher and harder challenges.

To test ourselves with progressively more difficult challenges, we have to start from a place of well-being. We have to develop a core set of skills that tell us when we have pushed ourselves to the limit and need to recover (and how to do it well).

The Foundations of Wellness

To reach and maintain high performance, you have a responsibility to yourself and those around you to take care of yourself. If you are at that level, chances are you have a leadership role. You're showing the people around you what it means to perform well consistently. And, as you might expect, what you do as a leader matters—for your performance and the performance of your team.

Research suggests that leaders who engage in self-care and recovery have higher-performing, more engaged teams than leaders who don't. A big part of this is modeling what it looks like to build a strong foundation of well-being that allows you to sustain performance over the long term so that your team knows how to do the same.[1]

This recovery time isn't time away from work, contrary to what we've been taught in our succeed-at-all-costs culture. It's an *investment* in your performance (and your team's) in the future. It's about building your capacity to handle stress and challenges and reach higher and harder goals.

Building adaptive capacity isn't about going as hard as you can all the time. It's about making sure you have enough in the tank, and that your tank is big enough to handle your toughest challenges. It's about being able to rise to the occasion. To do that consistently, you have to have the right mindset and consistently take care of yourself so that you can recover, improve, and iterate. Both mental and physical health are integral to peak performance. Let's start with the number one well-being and performance enhancer: sleep.

Sleep

Sleep is often called the best performance enhancer, but its reach extends well beyond performance. It's your life enhancer. While the general tropes about getting great sleep hold some weight (like aiming for seven to eight hours a night), there are other simple steps you can take to make your quality of sleep better.

Sleep is both a skill and a natural drive, like hunger. It's something you can practice, prepare for, enhance, do well, do poorly, or not do at all (note that a dire lack of sleep is fatal). But understanding sleep like this matters, because once you recognize that sleep is both a skill and a natural drive, you realize it's something you can train and improve. It's something that your body inherently knows how to do, too. This framing allows us to ease the pressure off getting a "great night of sleep" (a common challenge for performers) and to focus on building the skills we need to sleep well. That's good news: if you don't sleep well, you can change it. Now, let's turn to the fundamentals of great sleep.

Each person's sleep need is idiosyncratic. Though seven to eight hours is a great recommendation, some people will need a little more and some a little less. To start, focus less on the exact number of hours of sleep and more on how you feel after you sleep. A solid eight hours' sleep will generally lead to feeling better than a shorter or restless sleep, but track it for yourself and see where your energy sweet spot is.

One other note on sleep duration. A single night of short or bad sleep isn't going to tank your performance. The message that you need seven to eight hours each night to be at your best has become so commonplace that we've internalized that less means we have no chance to do our best. In my work with high performers from sports to business, the stress that accompanies getting one night of bad sleep is almost as much as the stress of the performance itself. This is your permission to not sweat one bad night. You may not feel your absolute best, but you can still succeed.

The next factor to address is your sleep window. If you're aiming for eight hours, but you get in bed with only enough time for six hours of shuteye, you haven't given yourself enough time to reach your goal. Your sleep window is too small and you're setting yourself up for a squeeze. That squeeze creates pressure to fall asleep quickly, which for most people has the ironic effect of preventing sleep altogether. If you want to make sure you get a full night of rest, give yourself the time you need.

The last set of sleep basics to get right is your sleep conditions. Set the room temperature at 66°F to 68°F (18°C) and make the room dark and quiet. If you can, leave your phone in another room. Limit your exposure to blue light before bedtime and give your body permission to do its thing and take you to sleep.

Coach's Corner: Tips to Improve Quality of Sleep

While a full treatment of the science of sleep would be too lengthy for this book, here are some science-backed tips you can implement to improve your sleep. These are the same tips I've used with pro athletes clocking thousands of miles, and I'm confident they can work for you too.

- Try to have a consistent sleep time (within a one-hour window) and a consistent wake time (as close to the same time every day as possible). Making sleep a routine skill to execute can help you perform it better.

- Avoid eating big meals too close to bed time, and limit your alcohol intake. Alcohol interferes with REM sleep, and as it metabolizes releases sugar into your brain that can cause you to wake up. If you do want to have a night cap, try to have it three hours before your bedtime.

- Have a consistent pre-bedtime routine. A pre-bedtime routine is the best way to prepare for a good night's sleep. Make sure the routine is relaxing, doesn't raise your body temperature, and limits your exposure to shiny screens.

If nothing else, give yourself room to practice enhancing the skill of sleep. Alleviate some pressure to perform and befriend sleep as an opportunity to get better and stay better.

Nutrition and Hydration

I'm not a dietician, so I'm not going to dole out advice in these areas. But what I can say is that there's a strong relationship between the gut and the brain, known as the gut–brain axis, which is influenced by what we consume. In general, good nutrition and hydration are non-negotiables for high performance, whether that's on the court or in the boardroom. Consume nutritious foods and drink fluids (as in lots of water) for a healthier life.

Teamwork, Connections, and Social Support

For the last several decades, Google has been a leader in the business world and an emblem of tech success. A company rich with data, it has set ambitious goals to optimize parts of its organization that an otherwise ordinary organization might overlook. One of those goals was to understand what makes a great team.

Google's Project Aristotle was an attempt to capture the relevant inputs that would lead to a whole being greater than the sum of its parts. This is basically the Holy Grail of teamwork. For companies and sports teams alike, getting the best out of individuals and the collective is critical to success.

The project began by identifying 180 teams—some that were high-performing and some that were under-performing. To no one's surprise, executives, managers, and team members had trouble agreeing on the factors that were most important in determining what helped teams rise to the top. Their initial hypothesis followed the traditional logic around team building: hire the most talented and qualified people, give them a skilled leader, and let them go to work.

Over the course of two years, with increasing frustration, Google struggled to identify what factors really separated the best teams from the rest. Failing to determine what aspects of team composition produced the best results, the company turned its attention to the intangibles. It looked at interpersonal processes, like the group norms, standards, and behaviors that held the team together. What the company found cut against popular beliefs and even its own predictions, and changed the way we think about successful teamwork. The best predictor of elite teamwork? Psychological safety.[2]

Psychological safety is the ability to disclose failure or challenges without fear of reprisal. It led to the teams being more vulnerable and self-disclosing, which increased connectedness. It also enabled the teams to more efficiently share and analyze mistakes, which allowed them to iterate faster. Rather than taking a punitive approach to failure, psychologically safe teams leveraged failure as a learning opportunity and iterated to make quick progress. The result was a dynamic team capable of self-regulating their learning, and a connectedness that allowed for real vulnerability and support from teammates.

That sense of connectedness is crucial for high performers. No high performer makes it to the top on their own. Every great athlete has a coach. If you want to be great over the long haul, you also need a team—whether that be your coach, partners, parents, co-workers, neighbors, or a stranger you connect with at the gym. We need the people around us to make us feel safe so that we can get energy and advice from more than just ourselves, and so that we too can quickly iterate on mistakes.

One of the most toxic beliefs we have is that of "individual" success. We celebrate leaders who seem to do it alone, and we discount the role their team has played in achieving goals. This narrative has been termed "heroic individualism," and it has the unfortunate effect of suggesting we don't need the support of others to be successful. We've been led to falsely believe that any person can be an island.

This view stands in stark contrast to what we know to be true about resilience and thriving. One of the most consistent predictors of our resilience is social support, whether that support is to help overcome physical injuries, like spinal cord issues, or mental health concerns, like anxiety and depression.[3] There's good evidence that our brains have evolved in size and scope due to our increasing interconnectedness during evolution. We need a community not only to survive, but to be well and do our best. Human relationships are so central to our existence that one reason scientists believe we developed language was to regulate one another's energy efficiency through communication. The people around us are powerful.[4,5]

Our teammates play a big role in our performance. Team members can help us learn quickly, provide us with diverse feedback, and help us overcome adversity. Both performance and wellness can improve drastically in the context of a psychologically safe environment.

> We need a good team to be successful. Teamwork is simply the idea of a group putting in a collective effort to reach a goal. We see the value of great teamwork everywhere in elite sport. Michael Jordan had Scottie Pippen, LeBron James had Dwayne Wade, Tom Brady had Bill Belichick, and Serena Williams had Venus. For an athlete to be their best, they need their team—whether that team is a coach or a peer. The team allows them to reach their full potential, complementing their skill set and serving as a source of support while sharing a common goal.

Stress Management

Stress is a core feature of the human condition. In its most basic form, humans experience two types of stress: eustress, or stress that is considered facilitative and good; and distress, or stress that is considered harmful. When we talk about managing stress, we're usually talking about distress, the kind which causes anxiety, pulls us off course, and drains our energy.

Unfortunately, some misperceptions about stress have become mainstream. For example, we're taught to think of cortisol as the "stress hormone" and are constantly reminded of how bad "high cortisol" is for you. You've probably heard that stress is as bad as sitting or smoking, and that your main goal should be a "stress-free" life. Yet, without cortisol, we'd collapse, with no energy. Cortisol isn't a bad hormone or even a stress hormone. It's an energy hormone, which kicks in when we're preparing to do something effortful. Arousal, the byproduct of cortisol, is a natural reaction when we are under "stress"; our brain is getting us ready to perform!

The way stress impacts us comes down to how we make sense of our experience—the framing and mindsets we have about stress. What we tell ourselves and how we understand what we're feeling have an outsized impact on our internal experience, overall health, and performance.

Kelly McGonigal, one of the leading researchers on the benefits of stress and author of *The Upside of Stress*, points out that we have a basic choice to make when we're faced with a stressful situation. We can choose to perceive that situation as either a challenge or a threat. If we choose to see the situation as a challenge, our stress can make us feel excited and ready to rise to the challenge, as if we have a superpower. If we see the situation as a threat, we tend to go the opposite way: stress becomes debilitating, harmful, and, if chronic, deadly.[6] This is the power of framing.

Stress Mindsets

The concept of viewing stress as either a challenge or a threat has led to some of my favorite research on what are called "stress mindsets."[7] Pioneered by Dr. Alia Crum at Stanford University, she's found that people tend to have one of three mindsets about stress that impact their performance.

The first mindset is the "stress-is-debilitating" mindset. The idea behind this mindset is that stress is *bad*. It's something we should try to reduce and get rid of, as quickly as possible. The problem with this mindset is that any performance or meaningful task comes with stress. So if you hold this mindset, you're likely to see stress as a threat and shift your focus toward getting rid of stress as quickly as possible rather than accomplishing the task. With this mindset, chances are you'll quit or fail. Quitting or failing will remove the stress but, of course, prevent you from achieving your goals.

The second mindset sees stress as something to "will your way through." With this mindset, once you're under stress, you just put your head down and power forward. I know a lot of leaders with a mindset like this—and it's often how we think about "mental toughness." What's fascinating about this mindset is that people who believe this don't tend to have much of a drop in their own performance, but their *team's* performance suffers. By focusing on just getting through the stress, they stop doing helpful things for their teammates. Since we're all part of a team, this kind of tunnel vision leads to underperformance for the group, which then hurts the individual.

If you're just trying to get through it, you're not able to help people around you do the same.

The third, and most adaptive, mindset is the "stress-is-enhancing" mindset. This is the idea that when you're under stress, it's a challenge to take head on or an opportunity to show what you're made of. People who hold this mindset perform better individually and as part of a team because they talk to their team in productive, adaptive ways that help their teammates see the stressor as a challenge too.

We should all be working toward developing this mindset about stress. The way you start is by changing the way you think about stress. It's called framing. (Later in the book, you'll learn more about ways you can use stress to perform at your best.) The more we can see stress as an opportunity to take on or as a challenge to overcome, the better we can be and the more beneficial our stress is. We can turn stress into a superpower with the right attitude about it.

Play

Adulthood takes it out of us, but it starts long before we leave college and enter the working world. With the introduction of No Child Left Behind, schools in America, much like businesses in America and the Western world entered the world of incentives and rewards, with a hyper-focus on achievement and productivity. The result? A dramatic decline in recess.

A study by the Center for Education Policy at George Washington University estimates that one in five schools has significantly reduced recess time.[8] In adhering to the edicts of No Child Left Behind and Common Core State Standards, schools began to systematically reduce the amount of time kids have left to play. In 1996, 96 percent of schools in the US had recess. By 2011, only 40 percent had an explicit recess policy.

The Western world's focus on achievement and productivity is slowly carving away at our ability to sustain ourselves over the long term. As the culture has shifted toward minimum standards, international competition, and teaching to the Common Core, play has declined, and alongside it, the well-being of adolescents and teens. Ironically, play itself facilitates deep learning and rejuvenates us—two things that would restore their well-being and allow them to be more productive.

Play is a primary technique for decreasing levels of burnout. When we think of our happiest moments as a child, those moments often center around novel and engaging activities with our friends. In fact, many adults report that these same moments are some of the most memorable and important experiences they have had in their entire life.

Play brings about several facilitative conditions for wellness, but none is more important than a full presence and immersion in the moment. Play happens in an unstressed, dynamic, creative frame of mind that's guided intrinsically by what's most important to us. It relies on exploration, self-guidance, and self-direction. Collectively, these conditions are a perfect recipe for restoring our mental and physical energy. Being fully present in this state is one of the most rewarding experiences in all of humanity.

Those who maintain a foundation of wellness are able to regularly incorporate play into their everyday life. If we look hard enough, some of the preconditions for a playful state—self-direction, self-guidance, and intrinsic motivation—are right underneath our basic daily activities. The routine nature of these activities blinds us to the opportunity to make them fun, but we can consciously decide to integrate a sense of play back into what we do.

For some, entering this state happens organically. Singing in the shower, dancing while working out, and playing with our kids can all bring about a sense of play and rejuvenation. These moments, however small, make us feel alive and good. Engaging in play renews our connection to ourselves and keeps the rest of our world in perspective. We can't afford, energetically, to be serious all the time.

THE ROLE OF SELF-AWARENESS IN ADAPTIVE CAPACITY

The starting point of any improvement is raising our awareness of the current situation. For example, if you want to lead your team more effectively, you have to understand their current strengths and opportunities for growth, as well as what would most effectively get them to their goal. Developing our self-awareness is no different. Much like a GPS, self-awareness serves as the starting point that allows us to determine the way to get to where we want to go and how best to enhance our well-being.

Dr. Tasha Eurich, in her book *Insight*,[9] provides a simple framework for building self-awareness. The first part is understanding the impact we have on ourselves. This means understanding how we relate to who we are. How do we talk to ourselves? How well do we understand how our values motivate our behavior? Are our values and goals interconnected? The more we understand these aspects of ourselves, the better we can map out what we'd like to change to reach the level of performance we desire and, more holistically, the life we're aiming toward.

The second dimension of self-awareness is the impact we have on others. We tend to underestimate the impact we have on other people. Let me illustrate with an example. If you've ever been in a romantic relationship, chances are you've sent or received a text message that says "We need to talk." In fact, reading those words right now might cause you to cringe. Almost universally, sending or receiving those words—even if we just need to talk about something mundane—is enough to spike our anxiety. The impact we have on others is far more significant than we appreciate, right down to the words we choose to communicate our thoughts and feelings.

This second dimension is important because most progress in our lives happens through relationships. Relationships are a cornerstone of overall health and wellness. Social support is one of the best predictors of resilience.

Belonging is one of the most powerful emotions we can feel. If we fail to appreciate our impact on other people, we risk draining not only other people, but ourselves. It's a vicious cycle; as we negatively impact another person, their change in energy is likely to cause our energy level to fall as well. Thankfully, we've got interesting research that also shows the opposite is true. Doing a good deed for someone else, despite the energy required, restores your energy.[10]

Growing Self-Awareness

To build self-awareness, we should start by working to understand what we need and value. Values are guideposts to follow to live our best life. The most important feature of values is that they should be action-oriented—something you can work toward progressively and never reach the finish line. For example, you might value hard work—and there is no limit to how hard-working you can be. Similarly, you might value kindness, and you can always act to be kinder.

These values serve as the cornerstone of a life lived "well." By aligning our actions with our values (we will discuss more on values as our North Star in Quality #5: Self-Regulation), we can bring a deeper sense of meaning and purpose into our life. We notice where we deviate from those values, correct ourselves, and move forward. We come to learn what energizes us and what drains us. As we build this greater awareness around a deep sense of purpose, our sense of what's possible expands.

The next step we need to take is to get feedback. We have to become aware of the impact we have on other people and invite other people in to help us learn about ourselves. The more aware we are of the impact we have on those around us, the more we build our awareness of how others impact us. This is a virtuous cycle. We'll find that we're more energized and connected in our relationships. And we'll also learn what we need to avoid that takes us down the wrong path.

Coach's Corner: The Role of Feedback in Self-Awareness

The main tool for expanding our self-awareness is feedback. There are lots of ways you can go about collecting feedback about yourself, and none is better than any other. The most important factor is gathering feedback from people you trust and whose opinion you value, so that it really sets in.

If you're looking for some tried-and-true feedback methods, here are the two I like the most. The first is a 360-review. This is when you ask people at work for feedback about your performance, typically including peers, subordinates, and superordinates. This process is best done with an external third party, like a coach, who consolidates the feedback and helps you process it. Having a coach lead the review also allows for your coworkers to be honest, without fear of retribution or needing to manage your responses. If you're willing to hear and respect feedback from a wide range of sources, this method can be good for you.

The second is to seek feedback from a group of mentors. Most high performers have someone in their life that they look up to, whose opinion they respect deeply—sometimes multiple people. Though it can be scary to "lose face" with this group, they can provide you with insights you wouldn't get from someone less experienced. If you can muster the courage to be vulnerable with this group, it can be highly valuable.

Armed with these tools, you can embark on a journey of continually raising your self-awareness. The more that you can understand your values, goals, behavior patterns and impact on others, the better you can adapt in your environment to facilitate long-term success.

Taken together, values-identification and feedback-seeking serve as the foundation for strong self-awareness. They allow us to be guided by our internal compass and to see how that compass impacts the world we live in. We gain clarity around our strengths and limitations.

Self-awareness drives our ability to manage and adapt ourselves in a changing environment.[11] Self-awareness is a crucial skill that allows athletes to recognize the psychological state required for peak performance and prompt them to self-regulate if they aren't in the optimal state to perform.[12]

The Johari Window

In the research on peak performance and optimal functioning, self-awareness often emerges as the first factor that high performers need to develop to succeed. It's at the start of a performance where an athlete needs to determine what tools they need to use. If they're too excited, they can only do something about it if they notice it in the first place. If their minds are unfocused, that first has to be noticed and then redirected.

But building self-awareness is challenging. It's often uncomfortable. To truly maximize our self-awareness, we need to hear from other people and get ready to embrace some difficult truths. We want to know where we thrive. We also need to learn where we fall short and how those shortcomings impact others.

Dr. Eurich describes self-awareness as the most important "meta-skill" of the 21st century and says that it can facilitate both survival and adaptation, as well as increased confidence, better leadership and performance, improved decision-making, and better quality of life.

So what does strong self-awareness consist of? And can we actually develop and improve that skill? A simple framework for understanding self-awareness is the Johari Window, which was "developed by Joseph Luft and Harry Ingham in the 1950s and is based on the idea that people can be classified into four categories according to how much they know about themselves and how much they reveal to others."[13]

The Arena quadrant is information known by myself and others. It is visible to all. For that reason, this quadrant has been termed "open." Our goal is to make this quadrant as big as possible through introspection and seeking feedback.

Figure 1-1: The Johari Window

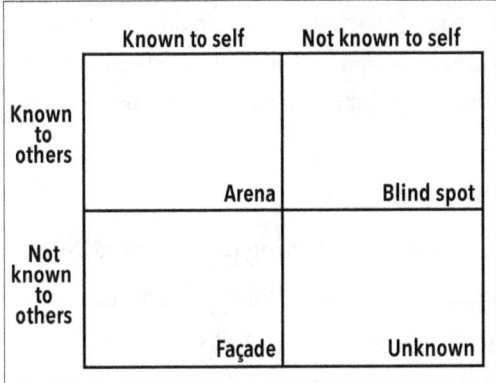

The Façade quadrant, also called "hidden," contains information that we know about ourselves but others don't. It holds information about our deeper motivations and values. We want to expand this quadrant through reflection and introspection and move information from hidden to open.

The Blind Spot quadrant contains information known to others but is not known to us. We should strive to reduce our blind spots by seeking and acting on feedback.

The Unknown quadrant contains information about us that we don't know and that others don't know. One simple way to reduce what's unknown is to actively experiment and seek novelty, and then reflect.

This framework aligns with Dr. Eurich's ideas about how to build self-awareness, which she describes as consisting of knowledge of ourselves and knowledge of how we impact others. She distills these concepts into what she calls the seven pillars of insight:

1. Values: Our core set of principles that we use to define ourselves and evaluate our actions.

2. Passions: What we enjoy spending our time doing.

3. Aspirations: What we'd like to accomplish during our lifetime.

4. Fit: Knowing what environments are best for us to stay happy and engaged.

5. Patterns: Our enduring thoughts, feelings, and actions that show up in the various contexts of our lives. We typically think of this as personality.

6. Reactions: Thoughts, feelings, and actions that show what we are capable of.

> 7. Impact: How our behavior affects those around us.[14]
>
> According to Dr. Eurich, our goal is to gain as much internal clarity and external awareness of these seven pillars as possible. The more we learn about each of these pillars, the better we can adapt and perform long-term.

Tips to Build Self-Awareness

If you want to enhance self-awareness, a good starting point is mindfulness meditation. Mindfulness, or the practice of being fully present and aware of what's happening inside us at the moment, can help us more closely attune to our body's signals and make space for new ideas, concepts, or values to emerge.

A second way you can build your internal self-awareness is to gain perspective. Zoom out and consider your life from thirty thousand feet. Imagine someone was writing a book or movie about you. What would the themes and topics be? What's the main narrative? What do you stand for, and who do you want to be? Answering these questions can provide insight into the way we see ourselves and understand our story. It can also illuminate gaps between who we are and who we want to be, spurring action and improvement.

Finally, though this list is certainly not exhaustive, having a regular journaling practice is an effective way to build your internal self-awareness. Specifically, you want to free-write for fifteen-minute intervals every day for several weeks, and then go back and look for themes. Recognizing these patterns allows you to catch habitual responses and to redirect when you need to. It also allows you to better anticipate and predict how you might feel in a situation, which can give you important information about whether to go forward or skip the experience altogether.

Even if we meditate, journal, and reflect with perspective with regular intensity, we're inevitably going to bump into our own blind spots. That's part of being human. The way to illuminate these blind spots is to build the second dimension of self-awareness—our impact on others—through external tools like feedback and coaching.

THE ROLE OF SELF-CARE IN ADAPTIVE CAPACITY

The final piece of the capacity equation is regular self-care. You need rest to grow from the stressors you encounter, just like your muscles need rest and recovery to grow stronger after a good workout. To facilitate that recovery, here is an evidence-based list of self-care activities you can do to enhance your capacity and performance.

Get outside. Humans evolved to be outside, and direct sunlight has several positive impacts on our well-being, ranging from regulating our circadian rhythms for sleep to Vitamin D to the stress relief associated with seeing nature. As a general rule, try to spend at least thirty minutes outside, three times a week. There are good data suggesting that this simple act can reduce our stress levels back to baseline.[15]

Be energized by the early morning light. Early morning light has several benefits. The first is that it can help regulate our circadian cycles; in the case of early morning light, it sends a message to our brain that it's time to wake up. Soaking up early morning light is a healthier start to the day than going through email or checking for text messages.

Find respite in the late afternoon light. After a morning in the office, it's common for people to spend their afternoons playing catch-up. It's draining enough without the glare of a computer screen and harsh fluorescent lighting. Even if you're working from home, it's easy to let the time pass without getting some fresh air. Late afternoon sunlight has two benefits: it creates a natural break point and signals to our mind that it'll be time to wind down soon. The late afternoon light sends a special signal that nighttime is approaching and starts to change our chemistry to support rest and recovery.

Exercise. Exercise reduces our risk of depression and anxiety, improves our capacity to manage stress, and reduces the risk of heart disease and other ailments. It's also a natural laboratory for testing the skills we discuss in part one, making it a great practice ground for mastering the tools you need to perform at your peak.[16]

Eat right. We know that a healthy diet is important for physical health, but what about our brain health? Current science tells us there's a strong link between what we eat and how our brain operates, just like there's a strong link between what we eat and how our body operates. Anyone who's ever used a wearable can attest to the difference in their "readiness" or "recovery" scores based on the changes in their diet. For our mental performance, a good diet helps us feel better about ourselves, reduces the load it takes for our body to digest food, and keeps our mind clear. This doesn't mean you can never have pancakes or ice cream; rather, it just means moderation is best.

HOW A PRO LIKE LEWIS HAMILTON BUILDS CAPACITY

Earlier we met Lewis Hamilton, the world's best Formula 1 driver. A huge part of Lewis's success has been how he takes care of himself off the track. *GQ* described him as a "world champion at self-care." He's the perfect example of what building a foundation of wellness looks like and how beneficial building that foundation can be. (It has led to seven world titles.)

Lewis begins his process of self-care from a place of self-awareness. He makes note of what his body needs and "how I'm treating myself." That allows him to determine where to put his energy to improve and where he needs some help. He then uses routines to ensure a baseline level of performance and well-being each day. Here are some of his non-negotiables:

- start the day by drinking water
- do 20 minutes of yoga

- do 10 minutes of meditation
- follow the daily training schedule
- eat a plant-based diet
- take naps

Lewis checks all of our boxes. He practices self-care, exercises, eats well, and has social support. This foundation sets him up to take on the most extreme challenges in (and out) of his sport. He makes a concerted effort to regularly challenge himself—to introduce himself to new challenges that evoke fear, like skydiving—so he has to consciously wrestle with his own limitations and build his capacity.

The best part of Hamilton's practices is that they're something we can all deploy. Any of us can develop routines that give us a foundation of well-being. Though we might not compete for world championships in our day-to-day, these routines can set you up to take on higher, harder challenges. You'll be in a position to think, feel, and perform your best.

* * *

Building a foundation of wellness is simple, but not easy. With effort, the practices I have described can help you level up your default settings, so you can raise your floor and ceiling. For sustaining long-term growth, there's no substitute for these core practices.

We'll now turn our attention toward the other psychological traits we need to sustain excellence over time. Some of these competencies will resemble popular twists on things you may have heard of, like resilience and grit. The first is mental strength. What my experience suggests is that many of the characteristics we require for mental strength—an unshakeable belief in our ability to reach our goals and in our signature strengths, and an internalized drive to succeed—can be trained with regular practice and pushing our limits.

ENDNOTES

1. K. Lanaj, A.S. Gabriel, and R.E. Jennings, "The Importance of Leader Recovery for Leader Identity and Behavior." *Journal of Applied Psychology* (2023).

2. Charles Duhigg, "What Google Learned from Its Quest to Build the Perfect Team." https://www.nytimes.com /2016/02/28/magazine/what-google-learned-from-its-quest-to-build-the-perfect-team.html.

3. F. Ozbay, D.C. Johnson, E. Dimoulas, C.A. Morgan III, D. Charney, and S. Southwick, "Social Support and Resilience to Stress: From Neurobiology to Clinical Practice." *Psychiatry* 4(5) (2007): 35.

4. William von Hippel, *The Social Leap: The New Evolutionary Science of Who We Are, Where We Come From, and What Makes Us Happy* (New York: Harper Wave, 2018).

5. Lisa Feldman Barrett, *Seven-and- a-Half Lessons about the Brain* (New York: Mariner Books, 2018).

6. Kelly McGonical, *The Upside of Stress: Why Stress Is Good for You, and How to Get Good at It* (New York: Avery, 2015).

7. Alia J. Crum, Peter Salovey, and Shawn Achor, "Rethinking Stress: The Role of Mindsets in Determining the Stress Response." *Journal of Personality and Social Psychology* 104(4) (2013): 716-733.

8. Center on Education Policy, George Washington University (2007 study).

9. Tasha Eurich, *Insight: Why We're Not as Self-Aware as We Think, and How Seeing Ourselves Clearly Helps Us Succeed at Work and in Life* (New York: Crown Business, 2017).

10. Lisa Feldman Barrett, *How Emotions Are Made: The Secret Life of the Brain* (New York: Houghton Mifflin Harcourt, 2017).

11. Natalie Durand-Bush, Joseph Baker, Frank van den Berg, Véronique Richard & Gordon A. Bloom, " The Gold Medal Profile for Sport Psychology (GMP-SP)." *Journal of Applied Sport Psychology* (2020). https//:doi.org/10.1080/10413200.2022.2055224.

12. Ruth Anderson, Stefanie J. Hanrahan, and Clifford J. Mallett, "Investigating the Optimal Psychological State for Peak Performance in Australian Elite Athletes." *Journal of Applied Sport Psychology* 26(3) (2014). https//:doi.org/10.1080/10413200.2014.885915.

13. "What Is The Johari Window?" Pelago Health. Pelagohealth.com/resources/hr-glossary/johari-window/.

14. Eurich, 34.

15. Jenny Brockis, *The Natural Advantage: How More Time Outside Reduces Stress, Improves Health and Boosts Social Connection* (Melbourne, Australia: Major Street Publishing, 2024).

16. Peter J. Carek, Sarah E. Laibstain, and Stephen M. Carek, "Exercise for the Treatment of Depression and Anxiety." *The International Journal of Psychiatry in Medicine* 41, no. 1 (2011): 15-28

QUALITY #2:

Mental Strength

Mental toughness and mental strength are the most important key factors for a successful career, especially for the long term.

– Roger Federer

Now that you're familiar with the basics of developing adaptive capacity—how to pair stress with rest, the foundations for wellness, and how to prepare yourself for higher, harder goals—what do you do when you attempt those goals?

The answer lies in what we'll explore now—*mental strength*. Mental strength isn't about pushing your way through things or trying to maintain some delusional level of persistence. It's about cultivating the right beliefs about yourself, through experiences and practice, to be bold enough to take on the challenges before you, even with fear staring you down. And it starts with a simple principle: the more you work at something, the easier (and less scary) it becomes.

HOW TO OVERCOME YOUR FEARS

When neuroscientists want to understand the brain's activity during a fight or flight response, they select a group of average people and, one at a time, encase them in a cold metal tube and flash disturbing images (think insects, reptiles and dizzying heights) in front of their eyes. Sometimes this goes on for more than thirty minutes. The researchers observe that the disturbing images cause several regions of the brain to light up because it is attempting to process the images and regulate responses. In a sense, the brain is under pressure.

The brain is reacting to unfamiliar stimuli. The novel stimuli incite activation across the brain as it reacts to whatever has come across the screen. The average brain engages in a flurry of activity to help these people regulate under pressure and stay focused.

I mentioned "average people" for a reason. When high performers get into the tube, their brains look very different. In one study, researchers displayed the same set of images to one of the world's top free-climbers, Alex Honnold, whom you'll learn more about in Principle #1: Preparation. Compared to average folks, Alex's brain barely registered a blip on the radar screen.[1]

Given that Alex defies death for a living, the results of his test were of little surprise to the researchers. They expected that images like bugs or heights wouldn't have much impact. After all, if you're not afraid of dying, what's a picture of a bee to you when you're in a safe space?

As they anticipated, Honnold's brain showed little response to the images. Based on past studies that indicated it's possible for people to not have a fear response, the researchers believed Honnold's brain simply didn't process fear. They concluded that his reduced activation allowed him to willingly free solo thousand-foot walls without a rope. But their conclusion was wrong.

That doesn't match Alex's experience. In speaking with Adam Grant on his *ReThinking* podcast, Alex said that he does experience fear, and regularly so. But since he's repeatedly exposed himself to unimaginable frightening situations in real life, seeing frightening or disturbing images from a safe distance in a metal tube simply didn't count as an activity that would evoke a fear response. He responds to fear appropriately for someone with his expertise. He is aware when there are real consequences at stake and not-so-real consequences at stake, as in a virtual environment. His mental strength is appropriately calibrated and called upon based on the task at hand, such as when he's three thousand feet off the ground in bad weather. Alex became an expert in understanding when to be afraid.

Through repeated exposure (the psychological process that underlies how we reduce our fears), practice, and repeated success, Alex built the cornerstones of mental strength.

Many of the characteristics we require for mental strength—an unshakeable belief in our ability to reach our goals and in our signature strengths, and an internalized drive to succeed—can be trained with regular practice and by pushing our limits.

Mental strength is the ability to withstand pressure (though it doesn't have to be life or death, like Honnold), persist at the task, and ultimately win. You could be pushing for a promotion, challenging yourself to make the next level in your sport, or trying to raise two kids under two. Building the strength to withstand pressure and persist requires self-efficacy (confidence), self-belief, self-control, and an unwavering drive to succeed.

Without mental strength, any (inevitable) adversity will derail your plan. Your performance will suffer, sometimes so much that it can't be turned around. Mental strength reduces the chances of caving in when you need to be at your best.

BREAKING DOWN MENTAL STRENGTH: THE TRAITS OF HIGH PERFORMANCE

You know mental strength when you see it. It's the athlete who resolves to not be denied—the last-second push across the goal line or the put-back dunk. The person who keeps showing up, after getting knocked down time and again. The single parent working two jobs to support their family, without complaint or acting like life is unfair.

When we see this level of excellence, we assume it's superhuman. That it would be hard to develop that level of hardiness to the circumstances around you and to simply keep performing. That people either have it or they don't. But the truth is, anyone can build mental strength with the right beliefs and psychological skills. Let's begin with confidence—literally, having faith in ourselves—the starting point for mental strength.

The Science behind Confidence

The first thing you do when you approach a new task is assess it. This process happens automatically and unconsciously. We ask ourselves a series of quick questions:

- How hard is it?
- What resources are required?

- How long will it take?
- Can I do it at all?

The answer to these questions hinges on our self-efficacy—how confident we are in our ability to deliver on the task.

Research into self-efficacy was pioneered by the famous psychologist Albert Bandura. What Bandura found is that self-efficacy comes from four sources, each of which we can tap into: (1) seeing someone similar to us succeed; (2) past experiences of success, termed mastery experiences; (3) effective self-talk; and (4) framing our physiology in a way that promotes feelings of confidence.[2]

When we have strong self-efficacy, we believe in our ability to succeed. We're confident and in control. We don't question our skills or doubt our capabilities. This leads us to take on bigger challenges, persist through difficult circumstances, and overcome setbacks. It also helps us perform better at the tasks we do take on.

Building self-efficacy is about stacking evidence that we're capable in a specific domain. It's not about feeling confident all the time—that's a wish that most people have but is simply unrealistic and, for most, unattainable (unless you're a narcissist). The best we can do is learn to accurately assess what we are good at and what needs work, and to account for the successes we have to build a sense of confidence in a task. Accounting for success is a step that often goes overlooked. We want to stack evidence to back up a belief that we can do what needs to be done, and do so at a very high level.

Coach's Corner: The Confidence Résumé

In my work with executives and athletes, I find one simple intervention tends to boost self-efficacy and help performers realize their full potential. This intervention is called a confidence résumé. What I ask these performers to do, and encourage you to do right now, is to look back over the course of your career at the high points. Identify your wins and the strengths you leveraged to make those wins happen. Then, go a step further and identify the skills you've developed between the big wins, and see how the wins have been a cascade of the skills you've built. This process helps people connect past mastery experiences with current strengths, highlights the skills they've built, and provides a sense of accomplishment that raises confidence.

It turns out that seeing other people similar to us succeed also helps us stack some of that evidence. On the playground growing up, if you saw your two best friends swing from the monkey bars and you'd never done it before, you'd feel more capable than if you hadn't watched a peer succeed. Your mind judges you to be similar and predicts you'd deliver a similar performance. This way of building self-efficacy is less direct, but still valuable. We're constantly comparing ourselves to others, so seeing other people do well helps us believe in ourselves.

The final two paths to building self-efficacy—effective self-talk and physiological appraisal—are also closely related. When you tell yourself that you're nervous about something, for example, you are more likely to appraise your physiology as a problem or a threat. By contrast, if you label the same sensations "excitement," you're more likely to see your psychology as helpful. This is a skill you can build alongside developing your stress mindset.

Self-talk can help you understand your physiology and position things more favorably in your mind. You're constantly talking to yourself—wouldn't it be nice if most of those thoughts were helping you, instead of tearing you down? Yet most high achievers I've worked with lead with self-criticism, mostly because they believe it'll help them avoid mistakes or failure. Unfortunately, that kind of self-talk can erode your confidence. Your mind starts surfacing doubts, instead of affirming statements of capability. If you can get your self-talk right, it can boost your confidence.

QUALITY #2: Mental Strength

Aaron Donald's Story

The best example of verbal persuasion I've seen is a viral video of Super Bowl champion Aaron Donald of the Los Angeles Rams. It shows him coaching himself before a big game, boosting his confidence by saying, "Do what you worked for right here. All that training you did ... is for this right here." He reminds himself of his capabilities, drawing on preparation, experience, and self-talk to feel confident and help his team win. Although the Rams didn't win in 2021, they beat the Bengals 23–20 in 2022 to win the Super Bowl. Aaron Donald is rightfully recognized as one of the best defensive tackles in NFL history.

To make that happen starts with awareness. You first need to catch yourself being self-critical. Then, in those moments, practice saying something more helpful to yourself. Your North Star is not whether the self-talk is "positive" at face value, but that it *helps* you perform better. With practice, you'll learn to talk to yourself in ways that boost confidence and, as a result, performance.

The last piece of the self-efficacy equation is making sense of our physiology. When our body is activated, most of us default to seeing it as a bad sign. The truth is, it's just our body tuning up to perform. Understanding our physiology allows us to channel that energy into a productive performance.

You can see what self-efficacy does for performance when you listen to performers like Alex Honnold talk about scaling rock faces with no ropes. To him, it's just another day at the office. He's done this so many times he has no reason to let fear overtake his confidence and focus. In an interview with *Harvard Business Review*, he said, "There's a brief scene in *Free Solo* where an fMRI shows that the amygdala in my brain responds differently than a 'normal' person's to low levels of fear stimuli, and most viewers come away saying, 'There's something unique about his brain.' I find that slightly irritating, because I've spent twenty-five years conditioning myself to work in extreme conditions, so of course my brain is different—just as the brain of a monk who has spent years meditating or a taxi driver who has memorized all the streets of a city would be different."

He's realistic in assessing the risks of his situation. He knows he can fall to his death, but spending any energy on a speculative result is a waste of energy and a distraction from the job. Besides, Alex has done this in the past—his confidence is built on mastery. He's watched his peers succeed, uses self-talk to assuage fears, and stays present to perform.

Self-efficacy—the science behind confidence—shows us that, to have the requisite amount of mental strength, we need to (1) believe we have the skills to execute, and (2) learn to embody that belief during performance. Once we've internalized that belief and turn it into confidence, it becomes easier to withstand pressure. When tension rises, we can talk to ourselves in a way that facilitates a focus on skills and execution, rather than wasting our time and energy thinking about circumstances we can't control. When our performance gets challenging and requires more effort, self-efficacy provides us with the confidence to rise to the occasion.

The Science behind Self-Belief

Self-efficacy compounded over time becomes an unshakeable belief in our ability. Athletes such as Roger Federer, Tom Brady, and Lewis Hamilton developed unshakeable beliefs at an early age that propelled them to the top. Tom Brady, drafted 199th overall (out of 256 total), told the team owner that drafting him was "the best decision you've ever made." Roger Federer wrote in a class project that he wanted to be World #1 before he was even on the ATP, at age sixteen. Lewis Hamilton has internalized this belief so deeply that he states simply, "I was born to race and win."

When we look at the best athletes in the world and what contributes to their mental toughness, the research consistently points to two unshakeable beliefs:

QUALITY #2: Mental Strength

1. The belief in their ability to reach their goals
2. The belief they have unique qualities that can help them succeed and that make them better than their opponents

These themes first showed up in a study where seven Olympians were interviewed about how they developed their mental toughness.[3] From an early age, these athletes believed in what was possible. That belief only strengthened as they progressed, and they built psychological skill sets that allowed them to maintain it. They learned to prepare more effectively and how to overcome adversity. They came to accept anxiety and recognize how to cope with it, rather than try to get rid of it. They mastered a focus on the present and what they can control. They embraced pressure.

Any of us can develop these same skills and, in turn, develop that same unshakeable belief. As Roger Federer said in his 2024 speech to graduates at Dartmouth College, this "belief has to be earned." It's earned through repeatedly seeing yourself work hard, succeed, fail, and iterate. As you make progress, it becomes clear that you have the ability to reach your goals, and that there is a special way that you are getting there. Over time, those actions compound, and an unshakeable confidence is born.

Coach's Corner: Sporting Genius

In a fascinating exploration of what makes for a "sporting genius," sport philosopher Joe Higgins identifies three key characteristics: creativity, risk-taking, and self-belief.

From Joe's perspective, the only way risk-taking and creativity have value is if the performer has the self-belief and confidence to attempt something novel and creative—to take the risk in the first place. He says, "Without a certain degree of self-belief, a genius will never have the ambition or assurance to rise above the higher echelons of one's sport; instead, the genius will be confined with others to the realm of commonplace sporting actions."

Self-belief is fundamental to rising to the top. Joe describes self-belief as the "justified confidence that one can succeed and choose the right action no matter the pressure, challenge, or obstacles of a given situation."[4]

In my work examining the mindset of the best athletes in sport, self-belief consistently emerges as a necessary quality for rising to the top. Oftentimes, these athletes believe in themselves before anybody else sees what's possible for them. Being able to recognize your own abilities and what makes you special gives you the fortitude and confidence to keep going, even when the upside isn't obvious.

The Belief in the Ability to Reach Your Goals

There are a few steps we need to take to build the belief in our ability to reach our goals. The first—as simple as it sounds—is to set goals and make a plan. If you don't take the time to consciously determine what you're working toward, you are leaving an important lever for high performance out of your arsenal.

The next step—monitoring—is fundamental to becoming an expert, but it's a step that many performers overlook. We tend to think of our goals as binary; we either reach them or we don't. Monitoring progress helps alleviate that issue by forcing us to examine what is or isn't working at each step along the way.

The reality is that most high, hard goals can be broken down into smaller sequential steps. If we learn to identify these steps and celebrate when we reach them, we build a history of reaching our goals and compounding our successes. Over time, tracking this progress gives us irrefutable evidence that we've reached goals and helps us to internalize the belief that we can do what we set our mind to.

This practice of breaking goals down into smaller steps also helps us to focus more on what we can control, which further facilitates this belief. Performance psychologists break goals down into three categories:

1. **Outcome goals.** These are the big goals you think of when you think of goals, like winning a championship or meeting your quarterly quota. They are the defined endpoint you are working toward.

2. **Performance goals.** These goals signal you're headed in the right direction and are a proxy for the progress you need to be making toward the outcome goal. If you're thinking of winning a championship, a performance goal might be to win 70 percent of your games. If you're thinking about reaching a quarterly quota, a performance goal might be reaching 33 percent of your target each month.

3. **Process goals.** These are the daily actionable goals you set to make sure you're making progress. It's practicing hard today, in service of winning the championship in six months. It's making all of your calls today, so that you can hit your quota next quarter. These goals are the things you can directly control that give you the best chance of reaching your outcome.

Research suggests that the more we focus on process goals, the better our performance.[5] An additional benefit is that the more you succeed in delivering on your process goals, the more confident you feel in your ability to reach your outcome goals. By zooming in on what you can do today, you believe more firmly in what you can do tomorrow.

The next step to take is to reflect on your past success. You had the opportunity to do this earlier in the chapter, when you were introduced to a confidence résumé. The confidence résumé is great because it helps cultivate belief in the ability to reach your goals and in your unique qualities that can help you succeed. There's no replacement for reflecting on past successes for building confidence in what you can achieve in the future.

When you take time to process what you've done well, you're building a richer mental model of yourself. Most people tend to focus on what hasn't worked and move on too quickly from successes. But in doing so, they've missed important lessons—namely, what they could repeat in the future to win again.

When you know what you did to succeed you feel confident you can replicate it. Your past successes are a testament to what you're capable of, with the right mindset and right preparation. Future success then becomes a matter of accessing those same skills, attitudes, and preparation for whatever the next challenge is. When you have a roadmap for what it looks like to win, you feel confident you can win again.

The final aspect of cultivating this belief in your ability to reach your goals is to build your ability to fully engage in your performance, win or lose.

When Roger Federer spoke to Dartmouth College graduates, he recounted an amazing statistic. He won 80 percent of his matches, but only 54 percent of his points. One of the greatest tennis pros to ever play lost essentially one of every two points he played. His secret to winning 80 percent of his games was to simply not dwell on the shots he lost. He said, "When you lose every second point, on average, you learn not to dwell on every shot. You want to become a master of overcoming hard moments. That to me is the sign of a champion."

What he's talking about is the belief that you can win the next point. And to develop that belief, he gives his formula that we can all follow. He practices committing his focus and effort fully to each point, and then, win or lose, repeating that process on the next point. It's a constant cycle of full engagement, completing the goal, and engaging fully again.

With repeated practice, Federer has overcome the same self-doubt and self-criticism we all struggle with. He had a history of being hard on himself, getting frustrated and smashing rackets when points didn't go his way. But to become an all-time great, he had to learn to let that go and instead recommit to the next opportunity.

What this process teaches is the belief that you can get the next one. Even if the first point doesn't go your way, the best thing you can do is commit to hitting your goal the next time. And, over time, this approach leads to a belief that you can apply this formula appropriately to reach your goals.

Federer sums this up beautifully as he closed out his commencement speech. He said, "The best in the world are not the best because they win every point. It's because they know they'll lose, again and again, and have learned how to deal with it." If you can develop your belief in your ability to deal with losses, there's nothing standing in your way of reaching your goals.

The logical next step is to believe you can make it happen when no obstacles remain.

The Belief in Your Unique Qualities that Make You Unstoppable

There's one thing that all sports dynasties have in common. When we review what's made them special, it always boils down to a specific "way of being." Interestingly, though, there's no one "right" way. In fact, two remarkably different "ways of being"—New England's "Patriot Way" and Golden State's "Warriors Way"—have led to remarkably similar results although by very different paths.

The Patriot Way is all about team football. Head coach Bill Belichick has regularly traded lauded players for younger talent that he believed would more closely fit his vision for the team. He felt his way gave the team the best chance for success. His approach was known for being calculated, critical, and demanding.

In contrast, the Warriors Way, led by their passionate coach Steve Kerr, is all about joy, individual expression, and connection. Kerr believes in enormous freedom, a commitment to keeping a team together for better or worse, and an emphasis on players being in control. In some ways, it's the opposite of Belichick's approach.

Neither way is better or worse. Both simply allowed for a full expression of the unique talents of these particular groups, and that full expression helped them to consistently compete at a high level.

The same process takes place on the individual level. Research confirms that a focus on our strengths and playing to them fully, rather than mitigating weaknesses, leads to improved performance.[6]

You hear this sentiment from the GOATs often. When they win, they don't talk about their opponent's weaknesses. They talk instead about playing their game and leveraging their strengths to do what they do best.

To do that for yourself, you first need to start by identifying your unique qualities that can help you win. Here's where your confidence résumé comes in again. You have written down what your past successes are and the strengths you used to achieve them. If you group those strengths thematically, you should have some insight into your signature strengths.

Another way you can identify your signature strengths is to ask people close to you to describe a time when they saw you operating at your best. When you get your answers, again, group them thematically. These themes provide insight into your unique qualities that allow you to be great.

When I work with professional athletes and executives, the confidence résumé and this feedback activity are some of the first interventions I use. I want to quickly dial in to what makes them special and figure out how we can align more of their time, energy, and role around those qualities. The more we can double down on strengths and move them in the direction of becoming elite, naturally the higher-caliber their performance will be.

To illustrate, a bank executive we'll call Sally came to me as she had just started a new role. She was moving to a new company in a completely different vertical and, in addition, was managing a team twice the size of any team she'd managed before. She was determined to make her first ninety days a success and wanted my help.

The biggest hurdle we had to overcome—and quickly—was her lack of confidence. Her past boss had absolutely crushed her self-belief. He would dole out harsh criticisms with no context, undermine her in meetings, take credit for her successes, and then privately berate her for not doing more for him. As she entered her new job, her sense of her unique strengths and what could help her win was at an all-time low.

In the first few sessions we had together, it became clear to me that her loss of confidence was driving fear-based behavior in her new role. She was afraid of giving tough feedback, establishing a new set of standards for her team, and speaking up in meetings. She lacked clarity on how she added unique value and, as a result, struggled to perform.

We set to work on illuminating these strengths as quickly as possible. We started with a confidence résumé. Sally surfaced several past wins, including running marathons, quick promotions, cutting back on bad habits, and building close connections that had lasted a lifetime. She then linked these wins to signature strengths, like her discipline to train hard for running and her work ethic to earn promotions. As we identified these strengths, we worked to find ways she could apply them regularly in her new role, from simple behaviors like getting organized to demonstrate her discipline to more complex behaviors like doing extra work before team meetings to show them she cared.

But what really seemed to unlock Sally's potential was the exercise of reaching out to close friends and getting feedback about what they see when she is at her best. One of her closest friends replied with a long note about her excellence, intellect, creativity, work ethic, and kindness. In an instant, Sally was brought back to earth and grounded in what helped her succeed. This same friend provided some great examples. Sally had solved complex problems during COVID. She had taken on extra leadership responsibility at work and in her community during a global pandemic. And she consistently supported people outside of her team, even if it meant extra hours for her at the office.

These behaviors gave Sally something to come back to and to adapt to her current circumstances. She started to make it a point to reach out beyond her immediate direct reports and build connections. She started to give more feedback to her team in service of helping them develop, rather than fearing their rebellion. Just a few months into working together, Sally's main concern around confidence was alleviated, and she could turn her attention to shaping her own culture to promote excellence in her department.

You can see from the example that when we focus on leveraging our strengths and see the impact it has on our performance, we grow a stronger belief in the value of those qualities in helping us win. And as that belief grows, we come to appreciate what we do better than our opponents. It doesn't mean we're better at *everything*, but that we have some strengths which, if acted on, can allow us to succeed in nearly any circumstance. In today's workplace, unlocking our potential is a combination of belief in our own strengths and appreciating what others do well. Other people's success becomes less threatening and instead illustrates what makes them unique. We believe in what we have to offer, and we believe that other people have something special to offer too.

With this belief in place, approaching challenges becomes much more manageable. When things get tough, we figure out which strength to apply and how to overcome any adversity in our way. We believe our strengths can help us win, because we've seen it happen.

Tiger Woods

The athletes we often consider to be mentally tough or the best competitors are the quintessential examples of commitment. To demonstrate, look no further than Tiger Woods. He picked up a golf club with his father, his coach, before age three. In his early twenties, he was already being talked about as one of the all-time golf greats, in the same club as Jack Nicklaus and Arnold Palmer. And, even after some self-inflicted adversity away from the game, Tiger vowed to return to his peak condition. It took some time, but ultimately, he was able to reclaim his spot as one of the best in the game. And, even when he wasn't at his peak, he was feared as a constant threat to surprise the field and win.

Tiger embodies commitment. It shows up in his game and in interviews. He has said things like, "There's always stuff to work on. You're never really there," and "I smile at obstacles." These are aspects of mental strength spoken into a microphone. Even greats in other sports have recognized his abilities. Rafael Nadal, in his admiration for Tiger, remarked that his face is "strong" when he's taking his shots, and that he's always admired Tiger's tenacity.

What separates Tiger from other golfers and competitors across sports is his attitude of commitment. His refusal to fall short of victory, to accept the status quo, and to never waver in his search for improvement are examples for all performers to follow in search of being the best version of themselves.

The Science behind Self-Control

Here's an example most of us are familiar with. We know intuitively that self-control takes a degree of mental strength. You might habitually reach for the ice cream at the end of a long day and, before you realize it, you've eaten a whole pint. This behavior is not a sign that something is wrong with you, but that your self-control is depleted.

Like a muscle, self-control is built through practice. And, like a muscle, self-control is drained as it is used. Some of our most famous leaders counteract that exhaustion by adjusting how much self-control they use for regular tasks, like getting dressed or choosing meals. For example, Steve Jobs' iconic turtleneck sweater was an attempt to minimize how much effort he had to spend choosing what to wear. Little bouts of using self-control add up quickly, but we can mitigate that risk by putting routine choices on autopilot.

Self-control became a popular topic in psychology since the release of the book *The Marshmallow Test*.[7] Written by psychologist Walter Mischel, the book highlights the outcomes associated with children who are able to control themselves in the face of temptation and those who give in (to see for yourself, type in "marshmallow test" on YouTube).

In this now-famous line of research, Dr. Mischel and his team gather young kids and a research assistant in a room with an enticing treat on the center of a table—marshmallows. The research assistant tells the kids she must leave the room for a few minutes. While she is out of the room, she says, they can eat a marshmallow right away, or not eat a marshmallow and be rewarded with a second marshmallow when she returns. She then leaves the room.

What unfolds after the researcher exits is equal parts adorable, genius, and fascinating. Only a few kids rush to get a marshmallow. Often, these are kids living in tough circumstances where items, including food, are scarce or taken away from them.

The kids who resist eating a marshmallow employ a host of distraction techniques, from picking up a marshmallow and playing with it to hiding it under the table and everything in between. When the researcher returns, their smiles are a mile wide, as they may eat not just one, but two marshmallows.

The researchers then followed these kids for some time, tracking a host of outcomes from academic performance to levels of stress and obesity. The data consistently reflect one finding: the kids who controlled themselves long enough to wait for a second marshmallow did better on all measures than their less-patient counterparts. So, what is it about waiting for a second marshmallow that ends up mattering over the long term? The answer has important implications for developing our mental strength.

Underpinning this ability to wait are self-control and delayed gratification. Self-control is what allows these young children to wait for an outcome that they really want and that is in their control, and to use skills to help them reach their objective. Though each child is enticed by the marshmallow, self-control allows them to stay focused on what they really want—a second marshmallow—and to behave accordingly, even if it means climbing under the table. And what motivates this self-control is delayed gratification, or the knowledge that waiting just a little while will produce better outcomes than plunging ahead straight away.

These two traits are inextricably linked. We exercise self-control in service of a larger reward. In the case of mental strength, exercising self-control shows up in avoiding distractions along the path of sustainable success. Those distractions might be the temptation to quit a task that is not going well, go down alternative paths or cave in to a persistent feeling that our time might be better spent elsewhere. Self-control and delayed gratification allow us to override those distractions and stay focused on our end goal and the best way to get there.

The Science behind the Inner Drive to Succeed

Any pursuit of excellence is going to entail ups and downs. Nobody wins all the time, as Federer showed us. As a result, there's a necessary amount of persistence required through the ebbs and flows of this pursuit. That persistence is behavioral and psychological; it's an inner drive to succeed. This inner drive encompasses several factors.

The first factor might be best summed up as an unwillingness to settle or accept anything less than the best. The best have high standards. Standards drive behavior and establish what we should be aiming for. These high standards keep us going, even when the game appears over or the sale seems lost, because we are committed to becoming the best we can be. The inner drive to succeed pushes us to work on our limitations and constantly strive toward being the best version of ourselves.

Olympic athletes consistently report that this inner drive to succeed is a necessary factor for the mental fortitude they need to succeed at such a high level of competition.[8] They visualize sticking with their goal and pushing themselves. As they make and internalize their progress, the drive strengthens. It's a virtuous cycle that allows the world's best performers to consistently reach new heights. As one athlete in one of the most-cited mental toughness studies put it:

> When you go through your sporting career, you have more knockbacks than you have out-and-out successes. I think it's those who don't quit, but who learn from setbacks that ultimately succeed. During this phase there were a lot of experiences of improvement in some areas, but also instances that weren't particularly successful. However, through reflection I strived to try and understand why the poor things happened and as a result increase the number of times where the good things happened. What went wrong? What processes or elements? Then, I'll go back in training and use this knowledge to motivate me to work harder on making sure that they were sorted, so I could be successful at the next competition.

To be clear, there are times when quitting is the right choice, such as when continuing would cause us clear harm or when our larger objective has changed. But, by and large, achieving anything meaningful over the course of our life requires a great drive to succeed.

The second factor is a growth mindset. In its original form, a growth mindset was about having the belief that hard work, effort, and persistence were critical factors in success.[9] You already know that you need to believe in your talent. You also need to believe that hard work can help you reach your goals.

As we pursue excellence, appreciating the role of hard work and effort in our long-term success becomes an important factor in staying motivated when things get tough. As it turns out, the more you appreciate the role of hard work and effort in your success, the more motivated you are to improve. As we see ourselves make progress, we start to increase our commitment to our goals, and we double down on the work we put in.[10]

In the case of mental strength, we have to believe that the work we put in is going to lead to the outcome we want. Otherwise, we'll just reduce our effort until we quit altogether. The added benefit of this belief is that effort is totally in your control. You can push yourself harder, dedicate more time or recommit a new effort to improving your performance. With the right mindset, pursuing excellence becomes about competing with who you were yesterday and making the effort to get a little better each day.

The final factor is a relentless pursuit of excellence. Some people might call that "consistency," but it's a bit more than that. For us to effectively ride the waves associated with performing, we have to have a high level of dedication to doing the work that will allow us to perform at our best. You have to be consistent at the right things, at the right time, with the right intensity. You have to fall in love with the monotony of training in service of becoming the best version of yourself.

The best only become the best with what Sally Jenkins, journalist and author of *The Right Call,* calls the "embrace of absolute drudgery." The best example of this embrace is the best swimmer of all time, Michael Phelps. The reason he approached his practices so tediously and maniacally was because he knew it was going to be key to managing pressure and the demands of the Olympics. Being tough in tedium was the only way to prepare for pursuing eight medals in one competition.

Phelps described his and his coach's approach like this: "When you're tired it's just sort of easy to fall apart. Over the years in the workouts, when Bob's gotten me to the point where I just can't move, he's demanded of me that I still do the right turns, the right stroke. So that once I do get to that stress level, I can still handle everything the right way and how I need to."

His training prepared him to handle harsh environments by pushing his body and mind to the limit. He'd train multiple times per day, all in service of becoming the best in the world. When he'd pass a milestone in practice, his coach would ask him to simply do it again, "just to nail it."[11]

This type of approach sums up perfectly what it means to relentlessly pursue the best version of yourself. Phelps was willing to do whatever it took, repeatedly, to win. But it wasn't flashy. It didn't require any special technology or bells and whistles. It was just consistently working on the right things, day after day.

Over time, the more we put in the work, the hardier we become. Practice, done right, strengthens our mind for the challenges of competition. (You'll learn more about how to prepare in Principle #1: Preparation.) We come to believe that our training is leading us toward being great at what we do.

The combination of an unwillingness to accept less than the best, a drive toward improvement, and the relentless pursuit of excellence are critical for mental strength because it's in the high-pressure, high-stakes moments where these attributes are tested. We need each skill in order to persist in the face of adversity, to not quit when it gets hard, to not fold at our first mistake, and to not settle for suboptimal when we know what we're capable of. If we're working toward a goal we care about, there should be little that can easily deter us on our path to mastery.

ROGER FEDERER: MENTAL TOUGHNESS AND HIS GAME

You can see how mental strength facilitates the greatness of some of the world's best athletes. Take Roger Federer, for example. A talented soccer player alongside tennis, he was forced at the relatively early age of twelve to decide which of the two sports he'd like to pursue if he wanted a chance to be great. For Federer, he liked the complete control that tennis offered, as well as the opportunity to rise to number one in the world. It also helped that he loves tennis—it's a game he cares about so deeply that he served several years as the president of the Association of Tennis Professionals to try and maintain the integrity of the game.

Federer embodies mental strength in action. He set a record for consecutive

Grand Slam appearances, pushing his body to the limits and his mind in the process. He also had to develop his self-control, which was one of the main factors holding him back from winning consistently at a young age. Rather than neglect the development of this crucial skill, he took to working with a performance psychologist to help him gain greater self-mastery. The result was a meteoric rise and landing as the world's best tennis player before he even reached his physical prime.

Federer was also known for leveraging other key traits for long-term success you're learning in this book, like play. His trainers were forced to make practice fun so that he could engage consistently and at a high level. Federer demanded that of his team because he was unwilling to accept anything less than the best out of himself.[12]

* * *

Just like our physical strength, mental strength is built over time with repetition. It's a skill. And just like our physical strength, there are different tools we can use to build different types of muscles. For mental strength to show up full force, we need to train our focus, commitment, self-regulation, and self-efficacy regularly.

Every performance we do presents us with the opportunity to build mental strength. No performance is ever totally smooth sailing. When things get challenging in the moment, we have an opportunity then and there to settle our minds and bodies, and to point our thinking, feeling, and physiology toward what's most important for us. We can practice controlling our attention and staying steadfast in our performance plan. We can choose to show up fully, even when it seems hard. And we can reflect on the strengths that allowed us to perform to draw on those as a source of confidence in the future.

Mental strength is an important psychological function. It arms us to deal with difficulty and to persist. But for strength to be effective—in other words, to perform at an optimum level consistently—endurance is required.

There is no such thing as overnight success in achieving greatness, no matter what our pursuit. It requires dedication to pursue that elusive goal we call mastery. What we can learn from elite athletes is how some simple practices sustain them for superhuman stretches of time. These simple practices can become our strengths too.

ENDNOTES

1. "The Strange Brain of the World's Greatest Solo Climber." https://nautil.us/thestrange-brain-of-the-worlds-greatest-solo-climber-236051/.

2. Albert Bandura, "Self-Efficacy Mechanism in Human Agency." *American Psychologist* 37(2), (1982): 122.

3. D. Connaughton, R. Wadey, S. Hanton, and G. Jones, "The Development and Maintenance of Mental Toughness: Perceptions of Elite Performers." *Journal of Sports Sciences* 26(1), 83-95.

4. Joe Higgins, "Why Roger Federer Is a GOAT: An Account of Sporting Genius." *Journal of the Philosophy of Sport* 45(3) (2028): 296-317.

5. O. Williamson, C. Swann, K.J. Bennett, M.D. Bird, S.G. Goddard, M.J. Schweickle, and P.C. Jackman, "The Performance and Psychological Effects of Goal Setting in Sport: A Systematic Review and Meta-Analysis." *International Review of Sport and Exercise Psychology* (2022): 1-29.

6. D.T. Kong and V.T. Ho, "A Self-Determination Perspective of Strengths Use at Work: Examining Its Determinant and Performance Implications." *The Journal of Positive Psychology* 11(1) (2016): 15-25.

7. Walter Mischel, *The Marshmallow Test: Mastering Self-Control* (New York: Little, Brown and Company, 2014).

8. D. Connaughton, "The Development and Maintenance of Mental Toughness," 83-95.

9. Carol S. Dweck, *Mindset: The New Psychology of Success* (New York: Random House, 2006).

10. Ayelet Fishbach, *Get It Done: Surprising Lessons from the Science of Motivation* (New York: Pan Macmillan, 2022).

11. Sally Jenkins, *The Right Call: What Sports Teach Us About Work and Life* (New York: Gallery Books, 2023).

12. Christopher Clarey, *The Master: The Brilliant Career of Roger Federer* (London: Hachette UK, 2021).

QUALITY #3:

Endurance

The last thing you want to do is finish playing or doing anything and wish you would have worked harder.

– Derek Jeter

In my research and coaching experience with elite athletes, one thing never fails to surprise me as to what separates the best from the rest: *There's no substitute for working really hard for a really long time if you want to be considered one of, if not the, greatest of all time.*

Leo Messi said that it took him seventeen years to become "an overnight success." Michael Jordan ascribed his success to the thousands of shots he's missed. If you want to reach a level of excellence at anything you do, you're going to need to be in it for the long haul. The psychological trait that facilitates this type of dedication is what I call "endurance." It's the ability to sustain long bouts of high-quality work over a period of time. It's about constantly working on your craft, year after year, in pursuit of mastery. Physical and mental strength will enable you to rise to the challenges on game day, but it is psychological endurance that sustains the drive for training over the weeks, months, and years. Sometimes, the challenge isn't beating your competition on the ice, field, or court, but just to keep going. There's a reason that the best athletes talk about falling in love with boredom as a necessity for rising to the top.

What we can learn from elite athletes is how some simple practices sustain them for superhuman stretches of time. People thought Tom Brady was out of his depth playing past age forty. He won a Super Bowl at forty-four. LeBron James has been in the NBA for more of his life than he's been out of the NBA and shows no signs of slowing down. Having watched him in person from the sidelines, I can tell you that even at age thirty-eight, which most experts would consider well past his prime, he's one of the most dominant players on the floor. To sustain that level of performance over time, he's had to work on his mind as much as his body.

THE BUILDING BLOCKS OF HIGH PERFORMANCE

Psychological endurance requires a special set of competencies and their respective skills, of which four are essential:

- Grit: a willingness to tolerate, and even embrace, discomfort and boredom
- Resilience: the ability to withstand stress over the long term
- Motivation: masterful control over effort
- Purpose: the ability to make something of each training and competition experience

These four competencies—grit, resilience, motivation, and purpose—are what keep you going when the going gets tough.

The Role of Grit in Performance

In my work with high performers, there are two drivers that are essential for building grit.

Driver #1: Passion

When the best athletes in the world talk about what allows them to show up day after day, the first answer they give is "the love of the game." Many of the all-time greats cite loving their sport as one of the key factors, if not the key factor, in their ability to persist through the otherwise endless slog of a climb to the top. Psychologists call this grit.

Originally coined by Angela Duckworth, grit is "passion and perseverance for long-term goals." In other words, it's pushing through the boring, mundane and uncomfortable in the service of long-term objectives. Grit shows up all over the behaviors of athletes who continue to deserve our admiration. In fact, in his book *The Art of Impossible*, author Steven Kotler identifies six types of grit:

- the grit to persevere
- the grit to master fear
- the grit to control your thinking
- the grit to be your best when you're at your worst
- the grit to train your weaknesses
- the grit to recover[1]

Grit has predicted success across a variety of domains, including military units, spelling bees, educational settings, and sports.[2] If you care about what you're doing and are willing to show up time and again, you're likely to get the results you're looking for in the long term. And that passion can fuel you through setbacks, allowing you to rebound faster when you've made a mistake. What you focus on instead is the deeper reason for pursuing your goals, and that gives you the motivation you need to keep going.

Passion comes in two forms: harmonious passion and obsessive passion. Harmonious passion is linked to doing activities for their own sake, because we value them and believe that they're good for us. Obsessive passion is doing activities because we feel compelled or forced and is linked to adverse outcomes like burnout.[3]

In the case of grit, we're looking for harmonious passion. This is the passion that the best athletes in the world cultivate, though they call it "the love of the game." It's that deep passion that allows them to overcome adversity and failure, to do the difficult work of refining their skills again and again. Oftentimes, it's this passion that leads to the intense emotional expression you see at the end of a championship. Seeing the hard work and care that goes into reaching the peak in something you love is a hard experience to replicate or comprehend.

The good news is that grit is something you can train. It starts by identifying your true passion for what you're pursuing. If you can regularly tap into that passion or your values, it becomes easier to sustain motivation when you're faced with the boring day-to-day. When you're at work and having the kind of day that you simply "don't feel like it," you can remind yourself of your values and what it would look like to show up as your best self. When you're making decisions about what to pursue and prioritize, you can ask yourself if the decision moves you closer or further to your thirty-year plan for yourself. That kind of perspective-taking and connection to your passion can make the seemingly trivial feel critical and more engaging.

Sometimes, passion alone won't get you there. You'll love the game, but you just "won't feel like it." When those moments strike, we need the second half of the grit formula—perseverance.

Driver #2: Perseverance

Perseverance refers to a set of behaviors we use to keep going. It's the proverbial admonishment to "keep showing up." And of course, the more you show up, the more likely you are to succeed.

Perseverance works well when it's done in service of something important or valued. This isn't about continuing to push for pushing's sake. It's about recognizing that, sometimes, to get through a tough period, the best thing you can do is just continue. We train perseverance each time we fail, get up, and try again, or push ourselves to the limits of what we think we are capable of.

Interestingly, one of the domains that reliably shows up as a way we can build our gritty persistence is physical training. And, when you think about what hard training looks like, it makes sense. Even some of the language of training mirrors the language of grit. We "push ourselves to the limit." And "you can't beat an opponent who never gives up." We are fueled by what it means to persist.

Physical exercise has a range of psychological benefits, but perhaps the least appreciated benefit is that exercise teaches you how to challenge yourself and to regularly cope with signals of distress, like an elevated heart rate. Neuroscience also reveals that regular exercise has a big impact on the energy we bring to the problems we have to solve.[4] In fact, simply doing load-bearing leg exercises was enough to grow healthy new nerve cells in the brains of mice. Exercise engages our full body systems and gets us used to coping with a big energetic demand, something we have to do repeatedly if we want to endure.[5]

We can also train our perseverance by reflecting on the consequences of giving up or times when we pushed ourselves further than we believed possible. If we can identify what's at stake or how we've persevered in the past, we can tap into another internal resource that can push us forward in the present.

Sometimes, perseverance is going to feel impossible. Your back is against the wall, there's an obstacle in your way, or something bigger is needed than just pushing through. In those instances, we need to call on an additional skill—resilience—to help us bounce back, and ultimately, forward.

Resilience

As a performance psychologist, stories of resilience never cease to amaze and move me. I've had the pleasure of working with some incredibly resilient performers. These are the stories that stick with me and shape the way I view what's possible for people everywhere.

One such experience happened early in my professional career as a sport psychology consultant with a football program. One of the most important players—the starting quarterback—ran into the room where I was meeting with the head coach, crying. I'd never seen much emotion from him, let alone tears. My mind started to race about what could possibly have happened.

He proceeded to tell us that his brother and best friend had been killed in gang violence. They were simply at the wrong place at the wrong time, and as a result both of them lost their lives. As the head coach and I sat with him and listened, the quarterback asked what he should do about the upcoming game. We were a small school and playing our only nationally televised game of the year in three days.

We set to work developing a plan. We wanted to make sure that he could be home for the funerals and that he'd have a chance to talk to family. We also made sure he had me as a resource and that he knew of other people he could talk to. He left town that night and returned two hours before kickoff on game day.

What happened next is, to this day, perhaps the most powerful experience I've had as a practitioner. Before the game, this athlete asked if I would pray with him on the sideline for his brother and best friend. Now, I'm not a religious person at all. But holding hands with this young man, our heads bowed, while he prayed before he played reminded me just how much people are capable of, and was one of the surest signs of courage I've ever witnessed.

He ended up going on to have one of the best games of his career, scrambling for an amazing 80-plus-yard touchdown run to close out the half and throwing several touchdown passes to win the game. Seeing him persist in the face of an adversity I could never imagine inspired me, and showed just how powerful mindset can be.

Over the past several decades, the idea of building resilience has grown increasingly popular as a solution to the exploding mental health crisis. We want to build a generation that's tougher in the face of adversity and more resilient to the stressors of the world; a generation that seeks growth, even when conditions don't support it.[6]

Thankfully, scientific studies of the best athletes in the world give us insights into the tools we need to build resilience and sustain performance over the long term.[7] These insights fall into four categories:

1. Clarity on what it means to be resilient
2. Refine personal qualities

3. Maintain a challenge mindset
4. Create an enhancing environment

Insight #1: Clarity on What It Means to Be Resilient

What the research suggests is that resilience can be bolstered in ways similar to the growth mindset. We remind people that resilience is about being able to withstand and maintain performance under pressure. It's not some mystical quality only available to the elite. With that understanding, people start to believe resilience is something they, too, can develop.

Insight #2: Refine Personal Qualities

Part of the reason we have to remind people that resilience is something you develop is that, when we see resilient performers, we immediately assume there's something special about them. True, they've had more practice cultivating the skills that lead to resilience. Bear in mind that resilience is a skill, and it can be built and refined with reps.

Let's examine personal qualities that galvanize performance under pressure. In his comprehensive research, Dr. Mustafa Sarkar, one of the world's leading authorities on resilience, has broken down these personal qualities into six components which, with effort, can help any of us to thrive.[8]

Component #1: Having a Proactive, Positive Personality

The first is what Dr. Sarkar calls the proactive, positive personality. Essentially, this personality is about being open to trying new things, taking risks, being optimistic, and seeking out challenges. It's about getting into the habit of doing more to develop in service of becoming the best you can be.

Performers who approach their specialties with this attitude tend to experience adversity as a sign of progress instead of a sign that something is wrong. And, because they are proactive in the way they approach their goals, they often use adversity as a mechanism for developing the next level of their skills instead of seeing it as something simply to "get through."

Component #2: Learning from Experience
Similar to building the self-belief you learned about in the last chapter, experience provides a strong foundation for resilience. Once you discover you can make it through an adverse situation, perhaps bruised but not broken, the belief and know-how to do it again become almost second nature. The most resilient performers make it a habit to reflect on their experiences, consolidating their learning about what's possible under pressure and then calling that to mind as they need it in the future.

Component #3: Having a Sense of Control
When people feel in control, the challenges they face don't feel forced upon them. Sarkar's research shows that performers who feel a sense of control over their performance and environments responded more positively to challenges they faced and were less discouraged when they hit a bump in the road.

Component #4: Being Adaptable
Resilient performers are more creative, open to change, and learn more quickly. In turn, they're able to deploy solutions more effectively and iterate based on feedback and what they learn. And, they are less taxed by the uncertainty they face, instead embracing it as part of their process of improvement.

Component #5: Having Perspective
How many times have you been asked about a test grade you got in high school or college? If you're like me, the answer is zero. But, at the time, those tests felt *so important* because we didn't have the right perspective.

Resilient performers manage to keep things square in their mind. They recognize performance as a part of who they are but not who they are entirely. They constantly work to maintain a sense of perspective that doesn't allow the performance to become all-encompassing, riding the highs and lows of each success and failure.

Component #6: Having Social Support

Finally, resilient performers have a strong support system. This support system could be family or friends, mentors or colleagues, or even a boss. What's important is that they realize they have resources beyond themselves that they can access at a moment's notice. This awareness allows them to tap into the people around them as needed to overcome obstacles.

These components form the foundation of becoming a resilient performer. But, there are other skills we need to cultivate to make resilient responding more automatic. Perhaps none is more important than the ability to appraise challenges accurately, or to develop what psychologists call a "challenge mindset."

Insight #3: Maintain a Challenge Mindset

As discussed in Quality #1: Capacity, people often think of stress as a bad thing, a chronic illness that can be as harmful as sitting too much or smoking. Something that can kill them. This is the opposite of a "challenge mindset." It's the mindset that stress is debilitating.

We need to learn to see stress for what it is. Stress is just your brain and body preparing you to do something effortful. It's like revving up an engine for the race. Your brain and body are getting you ready to perform.

Former elite athlete Dr. Alia Crum arrived to the field of psychology disappointed and disenchanted with the science's emphasis on stress as harmful or unhelpful. She set out on a mission to prove that the way we think about stress has a massive impact on the way our body responds. Over the last several years, Dr. Crum's research has pointed to a process called "reappraisal" of stress, which can lead to a host of good outcomes, including future growth, improved performance, and optimized physiology. And her formula for getting there is straightforward:

Step 1: Acknowledge the stress.
It sounds simple, but the default for most people is to try and run away or get rid of stress as soon as it shows up. Consistent with a deep line of research on experiential avoidance, Dr. Crum's research confirms that this running away only amplifies and worsens the stress we feel.

Step 2: Welcome stress.
This also sounds a bit out there, but bear with me. Welcoming stress doesn't mean we *want* stress. To welcome stress simply means we know that it's a sign that our brain is preparing our bodies to do something effortful, and we know that if we welcome stress, we can harness that energy to do good work.

Step 3: Use stress.
Now that we've allowed the stress in, we can use that energy to propel us toward our goals. This change in physiology, harnessed right, can motivate us to change behavior, persist in the face of obstacles, and work toward something meaningful.[9]

In my own work, I often add a step between step 2 and step 3, which is to see stress as a challenge. The data on the reappraisal of stress suggest that learning to view stressors as challenges—opportunities to demonstrate new skills, learn, or push ourselves—leads to "approach behavior," which is the opposite of the avoidance we mentioned in step 1. By actively practicing seeing stress as a challenge, we become more resilient to stress over time and train our minds to use that energy productively.

Insight #4: Create the Right Environment to Test Your Resilience

The research consistently points to three key features in promoting resilience that will show up again in a few pages: autonomy, competence, and belonging. These characteristics of self-determination theory give people a sense of control, enable a feeling of progress, and most importantly, help them feel like they belong to something bigger than themselves. When we're in environments that foster these three features, we feel free to perform, take risks, fail, and try again, without worrying about being ostracized, taken over, or feeling like a flunk.

Now that we've got a handle on resilience, we need to turn our attention to another aspect of endurance: staying motivated. When we work on something for a long time, it's normal for motivation to wax and wane. Deepening our understanding of what motivation is (and how to get more of it) can help make the lulls shorter and the highs more engaging.

Mastery of Effort (Motivation)

If there's one thing that precipitously declines in the face of boredom and stress, it's motivation. When we are bored or constantly stressed, it's easy to lose touch with what drives us. The day-to-day grind and associated discomfort drain our energy, both physical and mental. We go into survival mode, instead of long-term thriving mode.

The simplest way to understand motivation is as a function of the effort we're willing to spend. How hard we're willing to work is often in direct relationship to how important a given goal is to us. This hypothesis is called Motivation Intensity Theory.

Figure 3-1: Motivation Intensity Theory

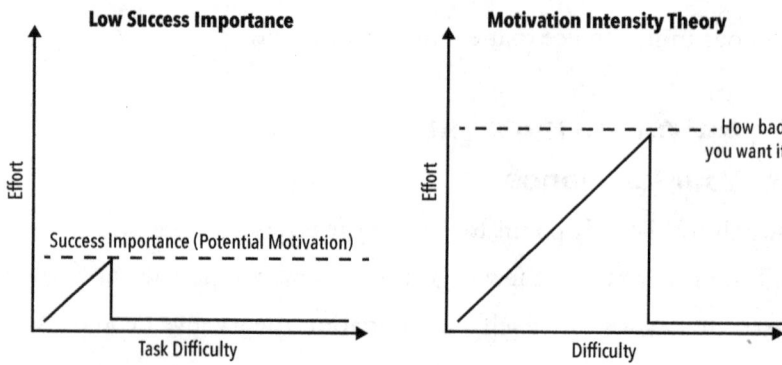

Here's a look at the relationship between effort, task importance, and achievement (i.e., the goal is reached). The higher the level of importance, the harder we're willing to work for it. If the bar for importance is low, and the task becomes difficult, we may just give up. This is part of the reason athletes stop pushing hard during regular season games. Winning in the regular season is important, but not nearly as important as winning games in the playoffs. Rather than push themselves to their full limit in important but not crucial games, athletes might choose to preserve energy for the next game or, in the case of "tanking," the next season. This phenomenon also explains a lot about human behavior.[10]

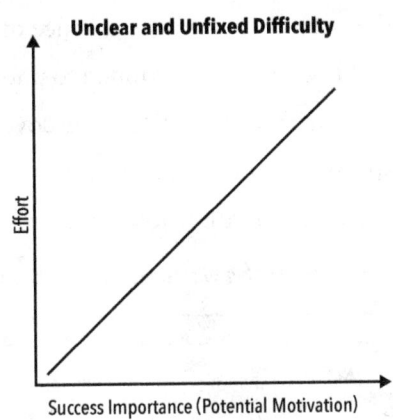

To sustain endurance, then, high performers need a different, deeper, more nuanced kind of motivation. If your motivation waxes and wanes based on the changes in goal importance and difficulty, how do you keep showing up to get better every day, even when you don't feel like it? What about when the goal for this year, like a sales goal or a championship, is out of reach?

Self-Determination

In the early 1980s, Edward Deci and Richard Ryan set out to determine what role the individual plays in motivating their own goal-directed behavior. They wanted to know: Are people more motivated from within or by external factors?[11] This was a different way to approach the science of motivation. Up to that point, it had explored factors outside of the individual, like pay incentives and bonus rewards. Deci and Ryan, correctly as it turns out, assumed that people might be induced by more than money; that motivation is more than a simple carrot or and stick (although it can be an effective tool too).

Convinced there must be something more—after all, people push themselves hard in the absence of an immediate reward (the carrot)—Deci and Ryan were determined to understand how people motivated themselves from within. What they discovered is that human motivation falls on a spectrum from intrinsically motivated to extrinsically motivated and not motivated at all. It looks like this:

Figure 3-2: The Motivation Continuum

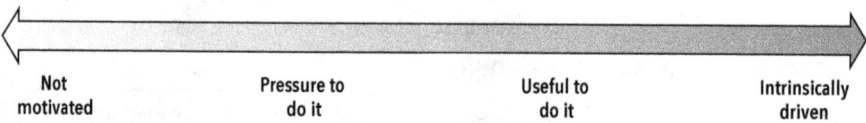

| Not motivated | Pressure to do it | Useful to do it | Intrinsically driven |

They figured out the formula for what's called *intrinsic motivation*, or the drive to do something simply because doing it is rewarding. The activity becomes a means and an end, all in itself. Since their initial study, these three factors have expanded beyond their motivational influence to be considered major factors in human psychology, from basic needs to general wellness to flourishing. They also predict the level of intrinsic vs. extrinsic (external) motivation, or the absence of motivation altogether.

People need *autonomy*, or the ability to determine what they are working toward—and how. We all want to be in control of our destiny. Having autonomy is about being able to determine the best way to pursue your goal and the freedom to determine what you're working toward in the first place. In the case of psychological endurance, autonomy may be the most important factor. We're much more inclined to spend long hours toiling away at something when we have the freedom to choose what to toil about. Being in control of our growth and development is highly motivational.

The second need is *to become competent at something*. People are inclined to keep moving toward a goal when they see they are making progress. Growing skills and taking satisfaction from doing so is a motivator to double down and train even harder. That competency can evolve into mastery is part of what keeps us engaged in difficult tasks like competitive sport for so long. Seeing ourselves make progress is a strong predictor of overall well-being, and making progress signals an important commitment to the task we're engaged in. As a result, we're likely to continue on that path.[12]

The third and final need is *relatedness*, and this need is likely the most fundamental. Humans need to belong, to connect with others, to feel a part of a community, and to be a part of something bigger than themselves. This is thought to be one of the main reasons the human brain grew so large. We needed more space and structure to accommodate the need for deeper relationships and social skills. This reality extends to modern motivation as well. We need relatedness to fuel our purpose, to make our effort meaningful. The human experience is vastly deepened by having people around us.

Think about the motivation athletes draw from being around their team and how motivating it is for you personally to not let other people down. That connection to other people and the desire to maintain that connection drive your behavior at work, home, and in your pursuit of achievement generally. We all want to feel like what we do matters to someone else, and we're more motivated when we know that's the case.

Since self-determination theory first showed up as a model of motivation, our understanding of these three needs has evolved so much that it's become a model of our well-being. The absence of any of the three factors is a major barrier to long-term health and a limiting factor to our full potential. Without them, peak performance is unattainable.

Purpose and Meaning

The final factors for psychological endurance are purpose and meaning. I've combined them because they are two sides of the same coin. Purpose is what gets you to the starting line and across the finish line. Meaning is how you come to understand how you ran the race when it's over.

How significant are meaning and purpose in life? In a culture that's largely oriented toward the pursuit of happiness, without meaning and purpose the experience of joy is a pipe dream. What does this mean for performers?

The Hedonic Treadmill

There's a nasty concept called the hedonic treadmill. It's the idea that we become less satisfied as we reach our goals and, as a result, we move the goalposts. This sucks the joy right out of working toward something meaningful. For high-performers, getting stuck on the treadmill is a natural consequence of losing touch with the meaning and purpose that started them on the journey in the first place.

An athlete I'll call Lucy was trapped on the treadmill when she came to see me. She was preparing for the 2022 Olympic Games in javelin throwing but was failing to progress in her sport past her last personal record (PR). She had a perfectionist tendency (as most high achievers do), but in this case, she was letting perfection—moving past her PR in practice—be the enemy of progress.

Lucy would go to practice and push herself more and more than the previous week. She was making consistent progress in her throwing, but it was never good enough for her. Rather than appreciating the progress she was making, her new goalpost was surpassing her PR. Anything less was simply not worth it. Burnt out by pushing to her limits without giving herself any reward, she started to stall and ultimately slipped backwards.

This pattern is common when you're on the hedonic treadmill. You get used to running nowhere fast, and when you stop running, you fall off the back. The end result is frustration, burnout, or worse.

We started addressing Lucy's performance issues by first returning to her passion for the sport. The best athletes in the world are motivated not by winning everything, but by becoming their highest, best expression of themselves. That's what Lucy and I needed to find. Why was she competing?

For Lucy, it was about representing her small hometown and showing kids what's possible if you commit to something. It was about representing elite women in sport. It was about seeing what she would be like pushed to her full potential. But she had lost sight of that and had replaced it with a poor proxy of a PR. Once we were able to bring it back into focus, it became easier to deal with the obstacles associated with her perfectionism and frustration. With a renewed energy for the game and a clear focus on her passion, she was able to ease the pressure on herself to regularly beat her personal records and instead shift her focus back to becoming her best. She finished the season qualifying for the Olympics, representing both her home country and her small town across the world in Tokyo. She found what you'll discover next—eudaimonic well-being and harmonious passion.

Eudaimonia

The converse to the hedonic treadmill is what is called "eudaemonia." In this pursuit, meaning and purpose are front and center.

The data suggest that eudaimonic well-being has benefits for both physical and mental health. People who pursue eudaimonic well-being through meaning and purpose experience fewer mental health symptoms than the general populace, can prevent mental health concerns from arising, and reduce the risk of physical health issues like stroke. And, they're better able to sustain motivation and performance over the long term.[13]

Pursuing eudaimonic well-being versus hedonic well-being is the difference between functioning well (eudaimonia) and feeling good (hedonism). While it would be nice to have both, the reality is that pursuing high, hard goals often comes with a great deal of discomfort and, occasionally, misery. Focusing excessively on how good we feel (or don't feel) in the context of performance is a recipe for failure. It's a distraction. Rarely do elite performers feel they can give 100 percent effort all of the time. The best figure out how to give 100 percent of whatever amount of energy they have left over, and understanding how to deliver on that energy is often linked to meaning and purpose.

With a fresh focus on meaning and purpose, we're able to make our daily activities impactful. A boring practice day gets reinterpreted as an opportunity to make real progress on a fundamental skill. The little things become big things when they're infused with purpose. Doing the same shooting routine day after day transforms into being a role model for younger players. Practicing the sales pitch for the hundredth time becomes a symbol of excellent consistency and a standard to strive for, instead of a pain in the backside to get through.

The Connection between Purpose and Meaning

In the psychological sense, a purpose is a "central, self-organizing motivation."[14] This concept has been around for some time and had several names, but the essence of the concept remains the same. The key features of a purpose are: (1) it's a core theme or aspect of a person's identity, and (2) it provides a framework for everyday life.

A purpose is similar to values, and I emphasize the role of values throughout this book. The key differentiator here is that our values guide the quality of our actions, whereas purpose guides our overall actions in a unified direction. For example, if our purpose is to be the best parent we can be, we can do so with actions that reflect our values of love, honesty, and dedication; but we could also have the same core purpose and be guided by a different set of values. A purpose is also different from a goal. A goal is a defined endpoint you can reach, and a purpose is something you pursue with no end.

Importantly, purpose is a key ingredient for making the most of meaning. Without a purpose, it's hard to meaningfully make sense of what we are doing. Are our actions taking us closer to or farther away from our purpose? It is a hard question to answer when we haven't a clue where we're going in the first place. There are three factors that determine the utility of a purpose: awareness, scope, and strength.

To be aware we need to ask: Do we know what our purpose is and to what degree does it guide our behavior? People unaware of their purpose often feel like they're simply going through the motions. Awareness of our purpose allows us to behave more intentionally, and to guide our thoughts and emotions toward helpful things that facilitate the active pursuit of our purpose. Without awareness of our purpose, we can feel unmoored and lost, and as a result, disorganized and inefficient.

Scope is a function of how narrow or broadly defined a person's purpose can be. The broader the scope, the more likely the purpose provides a coherent narrative and structure for a performer's goals and values. As a result, the person is more likely to engage in organized and deliberate pursuit of a purpose. If a purpose is narrow, it may influence behavior in just one context.

For example, you might have a broad purpose of becoming the best performer, partner, and parent you can be. That broad scope will help you find meaning in the things you're doing at work, in your romantic relationship, and with your kids. It also helps you make decisions—if an activity takes you in the opposite direction of one of those things, you choose not to do it.

A narrower purpose might be being the best CEO you can be. In this instance, you're likely to prioritize activities aligned with only executing a business, sometimes to the detriment of your partner or your responsibilities as a parent.

There's no inherent good or bad here, but it's important to recognize the trade-offs associated with each. A broad purpose is harder to pursue but makes for a more flexible, balanced identity. A narrower purpose is easier to pursue and might lead to more extreme positive outcomes, but can lead to more internal conflict when life throws you a few curveballs, and may lead to deeper despair if you aren't able to fully realize it.

The third factor is strength. How deeply connected are we to our purpose? The more meaningful a purpose is, the more motivating it is. How do we define meaningful? As we've discussed, it is the connection to our values. People with a strong purpose are more likely to persist in the face of obstacles, stay engaged with their goals when things get challenging, and find creative ways to solve their problems if it means making real progress.

If our purpose is weak, it's easy to walk away when things get challenging.

Now, you can have several purposes, but I'd encourage you to follow the Goldilocks principle as you explore. Too many, and you'll run out of energy to dedicate to all the things you're motivated to do. Too few, or none at all, you'll feel lost and your energy will be misdirected.

Finding your purpose can be challenging, though. That's where meaning comes in. What the best performers find is that regularly reflecting on what they do, and making sense of how they feel during an activity, starts to shine a light on the purpose that guides their actions.

Making Meaning

How meaning and purpose differ has to do with where they come into play temporally. Purpose lives at the front of the event. It's what gets us out of bed in the morning and helps us to keep going.

Meaning lives at the end of the event. It's how we organize our experiences and integrate them into our identity. It's how we make sense of things so that we know what to do the next day. Meaning is how we construct our world. Meaning is made.

Meaning and purpose have a bidirectional relationship. If purpose is the compass for our behavior, meaning tells us if we're following the right route. As a result, we can refine our purpose based on the meaning we make of specific things, and that refined purpose means the meaning we make of the next experiences will be different.

Psychologists have defined meaning as a "mental representation of possible relationships among things, events, and relationships."[15] In other words, meaning helps us connect things like cause and effect and to connect our actions, thoughts and emotions to our purpose. Meaning is an integrative process. The more that you take the time to make meaning, the better you can refine your purpose, and understand whether or not you're actually working on a task aligned with that purpose. To develop a purpose from engaging in difficult things, there has to be an opportunity to reflect.[16]

Unfortunately, our best examples of meaning-making often stem from tragedy, but there's an important lesson there. Take, for example, the heroic performances of the New York Yankees after 9/11 or the New England Patriots after the Boston Marathon bombing. These tragic events did not create a new purpose for the teams—they were both out to become the best they could be. But the team's continuation of play in the face of adversity served to make meaning, for them and the fans. Keeping the game going was a testament to the inability to dampen the American spirit. Fans openly wept because the games symbolized the resilience of a community and a country. Meaning emerged from the playing of the games that otherwise would've just been another regular season match-up.

The way to frustrate endurance is to engage our talent and energy in the service of something meaningless. We're human, after all. If the big-picture purpose is absent, it's only a matter of time before the other qualities we need to keep going slowly dwindle and we walk away. The beautiful thing about meaning and purpose is that they facilitate the other endurance competencies and skills described in this chapter. It's easier to maintain effort when we're working on something we care about. We can embrace boredom if we know it'll mean something at the end. We can persist in the face of obstacles if we know the obstacle stands in the way of our central organizing principle and achieving our full potential.

DRAFTED 199TH BUT NEVER DOUBTED HE'D WIN CHAMPIONSHIPS

There's perhaps no better example of psychological endurance than the leader at the helm of the storied NFL dynasty, Tom Brady. Drafted 199th overall, Tom Brady never lacked confidence, telling the owner of the Patriots, Robert Kraft, that selecting him was "the best decision the franchise had ever made." That confidence was backed by his passion, grit, and ability to extract meaning and motivation from experience.

Being drafted late was a sign that he was misunderstood and undervalued, in his eyes. It was another sign that he had work to do. When he was accused of deflating footballs and suspended for four games, Brady decided it was further evidence he wasn't totally respected. When he decided to leave New England, he made meaning of the experience by trying to find "joy" again in his game and to prove he could win a Super Bowl on his own. He did it just a year later.

But he would never have had the chance if it weren't for his grit and passion. Before he was drafted in the sixth round, he sat on the bench for four years at the University of Michigan. He was the *seventh* quarterback on the depth chart (an organized list of where players rank at each position) for some of that time. Most players I've worked with would've thrown in the towel, resigned to the fact that they'd never see the field. In today's NCAA, that player would hit the transfer portal in the blink of an eye.

Not Tom.

He waited patiently for his turn, eventually getting to start his redshirt senior year. It wasn't all positive then either. He split snaps with Drew Henson, another player who was revered as a better physical talent than Tom. His coach told him he'd play whichever player had the hot hand, which required Tom to persist through the starts and stops of being pulled from the game only to be reinserted at a time that may or may not be suited to his rhythm and game. Brady did it without complaining.

He endured all of that—and a twenty-year-plus NFL career—because he loved the game of football, loved competing, and loved winning. That endurance led him to become the definitive GOAT (for now, at least), the all-time winningest quarterback, and the most dominant player of the Super Bowl era.

I had the privilege of watching Brady practice with the Tampa Bay

QUALITY #3: Endurance

Buccaneers during the time the Toronto Raptors had relocated to Tampa Bay due to COVID. What first caught my attention was something rather unusual—Brady was taking reps at fullback.

I asked the person who had invited me to practice what was going on. Several of the other starters, including Brady's Patriots teammate Rob Gronkowski, were laughing on the sidelines. My host told me it was a rest day for starters. But why, then, was Brady on the field and lined up out of position?

Apparently, this was the new normal in Tampa. Brady insisted on getting reps to make his teammates better and because he wanted to win. He viewed each practice as another chance to get better, to prove the doubters wrong, and to cement his legacy.

Right then I understood what made him so excellent.

With enough psychological endurance, anything is possible. Brady's ability to make meaning of his experiences fueled his determination and drive for excellence. His willingness to persist, even when the signs seemed to suggest he shouldn't, facilitated an unmatched work ethic. And underlying each of those principles is his passion for winning and pushing himself to see who he can be at his full potential. This is what drives most of the greatest athletes, but to see it all the way through is a remarkable feat.

***

Though endurance skills can keep us moving consistently and progressively in the right direction, the endurance skills themselves are a bit fixed or inflexible. As the saying goes, doing the same thing over and over again and expecting different results is a form of insanity. Without flexibility, endurance skills start to look a little too much like the insanity we're trying to avoid. For us to stay fully engaged and successful over the long term, we need to be able to move more freely. Though we want to constantly make progress, the reality is that achieving our full potential looks a lot more like a mountain climb than a hill sprint. Sometimes you have to go back to go forward, go around to get up, or use new equipment to traverse an unforeseen gap.

For that to happen, we need the next ingredient in our mental fitness recipe: flexibility. Flexibility is the ability to persist, change, or evolve our behavior in service of our values while dealing with the difficult thoughts and feelings that are inevitable in the quest to be the best version of ourselves.

ENDNOTES

1. Steven Kotler, *The Art of the Impossible: A Peak Performance Primer* (New York: HarperCollins, 2021).

2. Angela L. Duckworth, Christopher Peterson, Michael D. Matthews, and Dennis R. Kelly, "Grit: Perseverance and Passion for Long-Term Goals." *Journal of Personality and Social Psychology* 92(6) (2007): 1087. https://doi.org/10.1037/0022-3514.92.6.1087.

3. R.J. Vallerand, Y. Paquet, F.L. Philippe, and J. Charest, "On the Role of Passion for Work in Burnout: A Process Model." *Journal of Personality* 78(1) (2010): 289-312.

4. Phillip D. Tomporowski, "Effects of Acute Bouts of Exercise on Cognition." *Acta Psychologica* 112(3) (2003): 297-324. https://doi.org/10.1016/S0001-6918(02)00134-8.

5. "Leg Exercise Is Critical to Brain and Nervous System Health." *Science Daily*; R. Adami, J. Pagano, M. Colombo, N. Platonova, D. Recchia, R.Chiaramonte, R. Bottinelli, M. Canepari, and D. Bottai, "Reduction of Movement in Neurological Diseases: Effects on Neural Stem Cells Characteristics." *Frontiers in Neuroscience* (2018).

6. Kennon M. Sheldon, Freely Determined: *What the New Psychology of the Self Teaches Us about How to Live* (London: Hachette UK, 2022).

7. Mustafa Sarkar and David Fletcher, "A Grounded Theory of Psychological Resilience in Olympic Champions." *Psychology of Sport and Exercise* 13(5) (2012): 669-678.

8. Mustafa Sarkar and David Fletcher, "Ordinary Magic, Extraordinary Performance: Psychological Resilience and Thriving in High Achievers." *Sport, Exercise, and Performance Psychology* 3(1) (2014): 46.

9. Alia J. Crum, Peter Salovey, and Shawn Achor, "Rethinking Stress: The Role of Mindsets in Determining the Stress Response." *Journal of Personality and Social Psychology* 104(4) (2013): 716.

10. M. Richter, G.H.E. Gendolla, and R.A. Wright, "Three Decades of Research on Motivational Intensity Theory: What We Have Learned about Effort and What We Still Don't Know." *Advances in Motivation Science* 3 (2016): 149-186.

11. R.M. Ryan and E.L. Deci, "Self-Determination Theory and the Facilitation of Intrinsic Motivation, Social Development, and Well-Being." *American Psychologist* 55(1) (2000): 68.

12. Ayelet Fishbach, *Get It Done: Lessons from the Science of Motivation* (New York: Pan Macmillan, 2002).

13. Richard M. Ryan and Edward L. Deci. "On Happiness and Human Potentials: A Review of Research on Hedonic and Eudaimonic Well-Being." *Annual Review of Psychology* 52(1) (2001): 141-166. https://doi.org/10.1146/annurev.psych.52.1.141.

14. Todd B. Kashdan and Patrick E. McKnight, "Commitment to a Purpose in Life: An Antidote to the Suffering by Individuals with Social Anxiety Disorder." *Emotion* 13(6) (2013): 1150.

15. Roy F. Baumeister, *Meanings of Life* (New York: Guilford Press, 1991).

16. Kashdan and McKnight, 1150.

QUALITY #4:

Flexibility

My mind is always free. My mind is flexible.

– *Eliud Kipchoge*

As a performance psychologist, the skill I train my athletes to develop that serves as an anchor to all other skills is "psychological flexibility." What this boils down to is being able to clearly identify and articulate your values, align your goals and behavior with your values, and persist as you need to pursue them.[1] What I find is that developing this skill allows athletes to adapt fluidly to the evolving demands of high performance and stay true to who they are and who they want to become.

Why are values so important? Values shape who we are. If we value being a responsible person, we make sure our promises are kept and whatever task we set our mind to will be carried out to the best of our ability. If we value being of fit mind and body, what we eat and how we exercise will promote our well-being. If we value family ties, then we will be there to help others, care for them, and nurture them. (Later in this chapter is a reflection exercise on values.)

What happens when we do something that goes against our values? This is different from questioning whether our values in the present moment are sufficient to lead us to our goals. If we do something that goes against our values, we will feel unease, anxiety, and guilt. In this book I talk a lot about energy. You can see how being aligned with your values creates energy. You can also see how feeling uneasy or guilty would hinder peak performance.

Flexibility allows the nonlinear path to peak performance to follow its natural course. Rather than expecting our performance slope to mirror the proverbial "up and to the right," flexibility means we can plateau, take a step back, go up, down, change direction, or stop altogether. The more flexible we are, the less we fixate on the illusion of a "correct" path and the better able we are to figure out what works for us.

In fact, this nonlinear path is exactly what real progress looks like. In their research on acquiring skill, scientists Wayne D. Gray and John K. Lindstedt identified a consistent pattern performers take in their development that they termed "plateaus, dips, and leaps."[2] Great performers often trudge along a path, failing to see any *significant* change in progress for some time (a plateau). When they look to make a major change, they enter a period of experimentation that leads to a temporary drop in performance (the dip). As they identify the new skill they need to reach the next level and develop that skill, they take a "leap" to a new level and start the process again.

The core premise of flexibility, in fact, is that it's about what works versus what's right or what's sanctioned. As much as we'd like a replicable path to excellence, excellence is idiosyncratic. The good news is you get to find your own way.

> The goal of all good performance coaching is to help take your ability to perform, in all circumstances, up and to the right. Coaches are important because they can help you identify blockers and limiting factors to your progress. They provide you with an outside perspective about the best way to level up and help make the nonlinear path more enjoyable. That's why the best athletes in the world work with coaches year-round and good coaching has become a part of the culture of medicine, finance, music, and more.

FLEXIBILITY IS KEY TO GOOD HEALTH AND HIGH PERFORMANCE

The science backs up flexibility as a key part of the health and high-performance equation. In one impressive detailing of the data, psychologists Todd Kashdan and Jonathan Rottenberg link this mental process to a host of positive outcomes, including:

- better mental health
- better physical health

- more adaptive pursuit of goals
- superior work-life integration[3]

And this is just the tip of the iceberg. In fact, the authors go so far as to call psychological flexibility a "fundamental aspect of health." Flexibility has implications for our creativity; thinking, feeling, and social relationships; and how meaningful we perceive our lives to be.

Studies have shown that psychological flexibility is associated with a range of positive outcomes, including reduced stress and anxiety, improved well-being, and enhanced coping skills. Indeed, Kashdan and Rottenberg presented the case that individuals who reported higher levels of psychological flexibility were found to have lower levels of stress, anxiety and depression, and higher levels of life satisfaction.[4] They also found that psychological flexibility was significantly correlated with better physical health, as well as improved social and emotional functioning.[5] (If you want a comprehensive review of the benefits of building psychological flexibility, I highly recommend reading the full paper. It's a long read, but worth the investment.)

We see psychological flexibility more often than we realize in peak performers. It's present when Naomi Osaka or Simone Biles steps away from the competition, when they choose a path that most people don't even see as an option, in service of protecting their health. And it's present in business, when some of the products we now know and love are changed for the better after acknowledging the original idea or concept was flawed. This requires letting go of the ego and choosing a new path that better serves customers.

At its core, flexibility is about adapting to situational demands, which means (1) being able to shift our mental resources such as energy, effort, and attention; (2) being able to change our perspective; and (3) being able to balance competing life demands. *If we can improve these skills, our ability to self-regulate improves significantly.* (A deep discussion of self-regulation follows in the next chapter.)

Figure 4-1: Psychological Flexibility

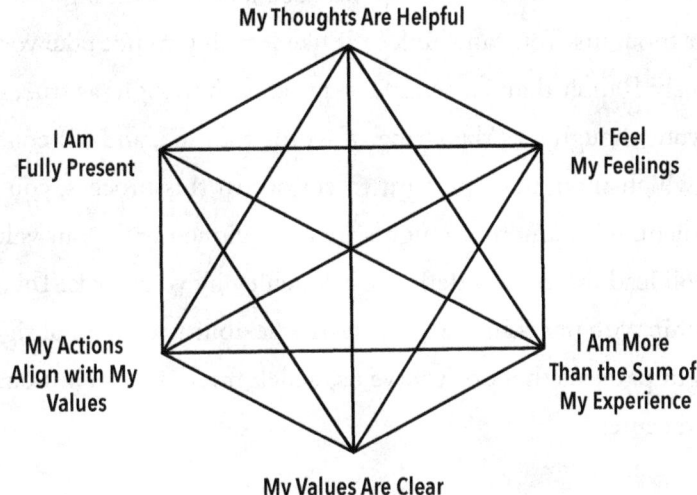

The ingredients of psychological flexibility enable us to adapt to situational demands. In Principle #3: Adaptation, we'll explore how it works. Right now we'll take a look at models of psychological flexibility and inflexibility.

My Thoughts Are Helpful

We're notorious for believing our own thoughts, even though we have evidence of being wrong quite often. (At least, I do). Defusion is a cognitive process that refers to the ability to "see" your thoughts in a more objective way and to make conscious decisions about what thoughts you act on and what thoughts you let go.

The propensity to believe everything we think is true or the way it should be is dangerous. We can all think of arguments we've had with loved ones when someone was unwilling to change their mind, despite overwhelming evidence of their inaccuracy. Though there are several psychological factors at play, one is the inability to, without practice, see our thoughts for exactly what they are: a stream of words our mind happens to generate automatically, based on our current situation.

If we want to get out of this trap, we need a better working relationship with our thoughts. You can think of it like learning to not take your mind so seriously. Rather than passively accepting each thought as true, strive to (1) see your thoughts as the string of words they are, and (2) consciously choose which thoughts you want to act on. In this process, you will be able to distinguish among thoughts that are aligned with your values and which will lead to, and not deflect from, achieving your goals. This type of relationship with our thinking gives us the flexibility to let go of rigid rules or thought patterns that don't serve us, which frees us up to put our values front and center.

I Feel My Feelings

This factor refers to the willingness to embrace difficult emotions while we pursue what's most valued to us. Emotions are often big blockers to our biggest goals. It's uncomfortable working on something hard, and we have evolved to seek pleasure and avoid pain. That recipe can lead to selling ourselves short, stifling our progress and, in some cases, can cause us to quit altogether.

Acceptance, like defusion, is about learning to change our relationship with our emotions. Rather than thinking of negative emotions as necessary to avoid, think of them as simply providing information about your current situation. You can choose to act on that information or not—again, based on whether or not an action is aligned with your values.

For example, when you're parenting, it's not uncommon to feel intense distress or discomfort when your child cries. That's normal! But if you value your role as a parent, then to do something less-than-effective, like ignoring your child (who obviously needs your attention) so that you can reduce your own discomfort will be an action that is not congruent with your values. Instead, if you accept the discomfort as a part of the experience of becoming the parent you want to be and relieve your child of their distress, you are matching actions to values, in this case being a loving, caring, and compassionate parent.

You see athletes working with acceptance of their emotions all the time. When you watch Carlos Alcaraz let out a yell after defeating one of the all-time greats, Djokovic, in Wimbledon, you see just how much emotion he was able to play with *during* the match. The big shout you see at the end is the final expression, but the feeling of tension, excitement, hope, and joy are there as he climbs closer and closer to victory. Each of these emotions requires some acceptance and extreme self-discipline to stay focused, not give in, and finish the job.

I Am More than the Sum of My Parts

You're more than the sum of your parts. At least, that's the basic idea of self-as-context. What this really means is that you are able to see yourself as something separate from the thoughts and feelings you have—you are more than them, and yet you contain them.

This skill relies on what's called self-complexity. The idea is that the more multidimensional our identity, the less we over-index on any one thing. It helps us to keep things in perspective, see things from several vantage points, and not over-identify with the challenges we face.

The importance of self-complexity shows up regularly in my work with professional athletes. When athletes or others performers reach a point where they consistently produce admirable results, their identity becomes defined by those results. This becomes a bit of a problem, because they define who they are by the outcomes they achieve. If they lose, they're a failure. If they win, they're superior to most. They lose sight of the other parts of who they are, like being a well-rounded person, a parent, or a sibling (to name a few).

It is one aspect of many that makes retiring from sports so challenging for a lot of athletes. It's not as simple as hanging up their skates and leaving the game. It's leaving behind a significant part of who they are.

This pattern is true not just for athletes but for performers in other specialties who have over-indexed on what their work means for who they are as a person. I have worked with several CEOs whose self-worth is almost solely determined by their business performance. Of course, so many factors determine business outcomes that choosing to wrap your self-worth up in something so complicated is a recipe for feeling miserable.

What we're trying to build toward is the ability to "observe" our own minds. We want to learn to see ourselves in all of the rich detail we possess—as more than an athlete or CEO, and more than the emotions or thoughts we have every day. If we can see ourselves from this observer vantage point, we can better manage the difficult moments of the day to day.

> I too struggle with this challenge. It's hard to imagine a life where I'm not working with the world's best performers, but it's always a possibility in a volatile world like sports.

Performers with greater self-complexity have a unique ability to appreciate the full spectrum of their human experience. This complexity allows them to nimbly shift priorities and coping strategies under stress, and to keep focused on their North Star without getting overwhelmed by their internal narratives about who they are or what they should be doing. Consider Walter Payton's reflections on leaving football, the Bears, and his fans:

> I want to be remembered as a person who, whenever he played the game of football, he left everything he had out there on the football field, did everything he possibly could for the team to win, not for himself. For the team to win.

> That's the way everyone should really want to be remembered, that whatever they did, they did it as best as they possibly could. That's all anyone should want in our life. It's not about being the best, it's not about winning this or not holding the record ... but for people to say, "While he was on the football field he gave all he had, and then when he was off the football field he was just that much of a person that you could relate to, that you could talk to, that he had feelings." That's what you want to be remembered as. Because football is a business. Walter Payton is a human being. If all I'm remembered for is a bunch of yards and a lot of touchdowns, I've failed. That was just my work. I want to be remembered as a guy who raised two pretty special kids and who taught them to be great people. Please have them write that about me.[6]

Walter Payton's North Star is clear: fatherhood. Being a relatable person. A human being with feelings, who can empathize with people from all walks of life. He is an example of being able to embrace the multidimensional nature of what it is to be human, which allows us to cope effectively with whatever comes our way. The narrative we have of who we are is richer and more complex. Our ability to appreciate the nuances of life is enhanced, as Payton demonstrates. He is able to adapt to life on the field and off the field, and always be guided by his values.

I Am Fully Present

The development of this "observing self" starts by training our minds to be in the present moment, usually through mindfulness training. In fact, being in the present moment and the three factors I just covered are all facilitated by a mindfulness practice.

The time we can be most effective in our lives is now. We can't change the past and have little to no ability to accurately predict the future, including what we'll think or how we'll feel. The best we can do is to be fully here now and to choose to align our actions with our values. If you can be fully present, you give yourself the best chance of bringing your ideal future to life by doing what's most effective at any given moment.

Coach's Corner: Leaves on a Stream

Learning to meditate can be intimidating. One of my favorite exercises to start with is called Leaves on a Stream, and you can try it right now. Read these instructions all the way through and then begin.

Close your eyes and bring your attention to your breathing. Notice the in-breath and out-breath, and how the breath feels going in and out through your nose.

As thoughts arise, I want you to imagine them floating gently by, like leaves on a stream. Place a thought on a leaf and notice how it passes by, without getting attached. Repeat this exercise for five minutes, simply noticing and letting go of thoughts as they come and go.

My Values Are Clear

Values, in the context of psychological flexibility, are *mental representations* of the characteristics we want to embody. Put more simply, they're just words that we are trying to bring to life. But words have a powerful ability to guide our behavior.

For a moment, I want you to imagine your funeral. A bit morbid, I know, but bear with me. Imagine that your best friend and partner get up to talk about you in front of all your family and friends. What would you want them to say about you?

Chances are, you're like Walter Payton. You're not interested in them talking about how many meetings you attended or how many games you played. You want them to talk about what you meant to them. About what you represented. About the type of person you were.

You want them to say things like you were loving, compassionate, hardworking, determined, and a kind person. These concepts are your values.

They represent your idealized future self, the person you want to become, and the guardrails as you work toward achieving your goals. These values serve as your guide for a rich, meaningful life.

My Actions Align with My Values

Ben Franklin used to keep track of his thirteen values in a notebook. Each day, he would score himself according to how closely he aligned his actions with those values. He consciously tracked becoming the person he wanted to be, day by day. Though you don't have to do this as meticulously as Ben, it's a great way to hold yourself accountable to living those values. And the side effects of doing so are all positive: more confidence, a more meaningful life, and a deeper sense of purpose.

This is what it means to take committed action. You match your actions and daily habits to your values, and you get after your goals by embracing difficult emotions and throwing self-doubt out the window. Committed action is about understanding that the only way to bring your values to life is to *live* them, moment to moment, and day to day.

Committed action also gives us a straightforward guide to what we should do at any given moment. What value matters most in this situation, and what would it look like to act on that? Choosing to act is taking committed action. And what we know is that, over time, the more you engage in life this way, the better you'll feel and the more you'll achieve.

There is an aspect of human nature that can derail committed action. We tend to want to avoid discomfort. It might even be an evolutionary tendency to back away from things that might result in injury or worse. Avoidance, as you can guess, can move us away from peak performance.

The Dilemma of Avoidance: Psychological Inflexibility

At the core of psychological inflexibility is a process that psychologists call "avoidance." Avoidance is as it sounds—people actively avoid things that create discomfort. Some speculate that this avoidance is a product of our culture's emphasis on the pursuit of happiness, but what we've found is that avoidance is a surefire way to make your life decidedly not happy. The more you avoid, the smaller and more superficial your world gets.[7]

Figure 4-2: Psychological Inflexibility

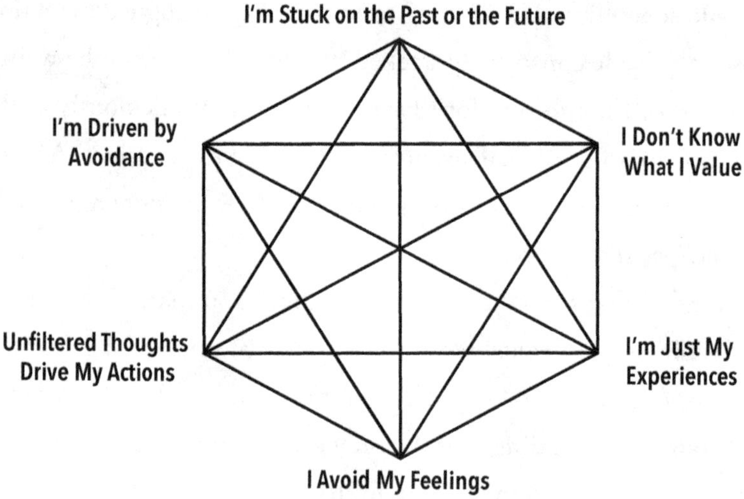

```
                    I'm Stuck on the Past or the Future

     I'm Driven by                                    I Don't Know
     Avoidance                                        What I Value



     Unfiltered Thoughts                              I'm Just My
     Drive My Actions                                 Experiences

                         I Avoid My Feelings
```

I'm Stuck on the Past or the Future

If you are spending too much time in the "woulda shoulda zone," you're not only wasting your time, but worse, the world is passing you by. If you have challenges to address and goals to achieve you must be fully present. Meeting challenges and achieving goals is done by applying your values to the work at hand. Avoidance is impossible if you want to get something important done.

I Don't Know What I Value

It is safe to say that if you don't know what you value, you have not thought hard enough about your identity and how you are showing up in the world. Performance at any level is impossible without values to back up your behaviors and actions. Read Walter Payton's words again. What resonates with you? Think of teachers you respect and other role models who have made a difference in your life? What characteristics and traits have stayed in your mind? Which ones do you choose to emulate?

I'm Just My Experience

As you read in the section "I Am More than the Sum of My Parts," your sense of self-worth can be damaged by not seeing yourself as the person you really are. People define themselves in ways that fail to convey the entirety of who they are. As I said, athletes define themselves by their ability on the field of play and businesspeople by their quarterly earnings. You need to see yourself in all of the rich detail that makes you who you are. By telling this story, you'll be able to cope with whatever comes your way.

I Avoid My Feelings

Painful emotions can put up barriers to moving forward. But there is no other way. You must change your relationship with your emotions. My advice is to think of emotions like pieces of information or bits of data. Information and data are useful. Ask yourself, "Why am I feeling this way?" and "What other ways can I look at this problem without so much emotion attached to it?" Asking questions brings clarity and just may bring down the temperature too.

Unfiltered Thoughts Drive My Actions

We are all guilty of making knee-jerk responses to comments we disagree with or that don't match our way of thinking. In both cases, if we were to reflect on what we heard and were not so quick to open our mouth, our response might be different and perhaps more meaningful and better aligned with our values. The relationship between mind and mouth is really about self-discipline, which is fundamental to performance.

I'm Driven by Avoidance

It might be the case that you didn't have name for what is holding you back or for your inability to commit to taking action. The factors I see are, in summation, failing to be present and have presence of mind; not knowing your values, which guide actions; underestimating your skills and talent; not being able to deal with emotions; and failing to exercise self-discipline.

Think about the pro athlete who experiences some performance anxiety. What would be the fastest way for them to get rid of that? Not show up at all! If we all just avoided things that made us uncomfortable, nothing great would happen. But, we have to consciously override our tendency to choose comfort over growth. We have to motivate ourselves to be better than we are today and to push ourselves to our limits.

Avoidance can take many forms. We might avoid certain thoughts or feelings, or we might avoid taking decisive, committed action because we are afraid of the consequences. You've likely seen avoidance come up in yourself or others. It looks like the person who's reluctant to go to the party because they fear how they'll be judged (avoiding fear) or who plays video games instead of doing the work they need to do to prepare for a big presentation. What happens when people avoid doing something over time is like an avoidance scope creep. Things that once weren't so intimidating loom larger and larger, and do so until the person is afraid to leave their house because a stranger might judge them.

> There are going to be times when performers must take the risk that they might fail. Avoidance would suggest that you back down at the moment of the choice and preserve your sense of safety and security. In contrast, adaptation demands psychological flexibility—the ability to be present with your discomfort and do what you need to do to reach your goals.

A TALE OF TWO COACHES: FLEXIBILITY—A WINNING FORMULA

There's an old saying in the sports world: "Coach the players you have, not the players you want." Coaches who focus too much on the latter risk having their tenure cut short. Those who are able to consistently adapt to the competitive landscape and team composition are able to win year after year.

Perhaps there are no better examples of this capability than two of the all-time great football coaches, who also happen to be close friends: Bill Belichick and Nick Saban.

These two coaches are known for building dynasties at their respective levels. The New England Patriots and the University of Alabama Crimson Tide had (or in the case of Alabama, continue to have) nearly a decade of unparalleled success, despite the frequent turnover of players and staff. Alabama gets a new roster every four years and NFL teams regularly cherry-pick the Patriots' coaches.

What allowed these coaches and their teams to maintain this level of success was their flexibility. They didn't get too attached to their team identities or resist changing the way they played from year to year. Instead, they both evolved their systems to fit the players on the roster. They were guided by their values and philosophies, and adapted their systems to best fit the players. The end result was consistently putting their players in a position to be the best they could be, and as a result, putting the team in a position to win (committed action aligned with their core values).

This required the teams to expand their identities, both on and off the field. In today's college football, for example, the Name, Image, and Likeness legislation necessitated a change in the way Alabama recruits football players. Though Alabama's reputation remains stellar and the school continues to attract high-quality prospects, they've also adapted their approach to show that they're attuned to the needs of high school athletes. They deploy new recruiting strategies off the field to secure better talent, and new plays on the field to help that talent reach their full potential.

Finally, both teams adjust and respond regularly to feedback. In a team sport like football, feedback happens often—we know the outcome of each play, and we also know the outcome of a game. Winning and losing are essentially feedback mechanisms that allow coaches to determine if they should desist or persist in a given strategy. They use the emotions and thoughts associated with winning and losing to effectively serve their ends—winning more games—but don't hold onto the wins or losses. In fact, Saban famously only lets his staff celebrate a national championship for twenty-four hours before they get back to learning about what adaptation is next.

These teams are known for approaching each game as a unique competition, because no two competitors are alike and sticking strictly to one offensive playbook and one defensive playbook will have its drawbacks. Flexibility is required during the week's practice before game day and during the game itself. The Crimson Tide and the Patriots will change their tactics when they're not making headway against the opposing team. Rather than mindlessly sticking to a script they thought would be successful based on scouting reports, they adapt in the moment. Importantly, too, though both teams are known for their winning ways, they don't take success as a sign to just stay the same. They constantly evolve for greater chances of success.

* * *

Flexibility is a cornerstone of fulfilling your potential. The data are clear: building psychological flexibility not only enhances your mental health and performance but is essential for your physical and social health as well. It's also the building block for what I call the pivot point between mental strength and a state of well-being and aspiring to become a peak performer.

QUALITY #4: Flexibility

In the final chapter of part one, we discuss self-regulation. It is our ability to master our thoughts, emotions, and behaviors in pursuit of our goals. Self-regulation at a high level means we have the opportunity to live well and perform well.

ENDNOTES

1. James D. Dooley, Fallon R. Goodman, and Todd B. Kashdan, "Psychological Flexibility: What We Know, What We Do Not Know, and What We Think We Know." *Social and Psychology Compass* 14(12) (2020): 1-11. https://doi.org/10.1111/spc3.12566.

2. Wayne D. Gray and John K. Lindstedt, "Plateaus, Dips and Leaps: Where to Look for Inventions and Discoveries During Skilled Performance." *Cognitive Science* 41 (2017): 1838-1870.

3. Todd B. Kashdan and Jonathan Rottenberg, "Psychological Flexibility as an Aspect of Health." *Clinical Psychology Review* 30(7) (2010): 865-878. https://doi.org/10.1016/j.cpr. 2010.03.001.

4. Kashdan and Rottenberg, 865-878.

5. Kashdan and Rottenberg, 865-878.

6. Walter Payton with Don Yaeger, Never Die Easy: The Autobiography of Walter Payton (New York: Villard Books, 2000): 248-249.

7. Michael E. Levin et al., "Examining Psychological Inflexibility as a Transdiagnostic Process across Psychological Disorders." *Journal of Contextual Behavioral Science* 3(3) (2014): 155-163.

QUALITY #5:

Self-Regulation

Tennis is a mental game. You have to stay focused and controlled. You have to adapt to different playing styles and conditions.

– Roger Federer

When you hear talk of excellence, you hear one word more than others: mastery. The all-time greats tend to focus on mastering themselves. Michael Jordan, in *The Last Dance*, talks about focusing on becoming the best player he could be. When Tom Brady left the New England Patriots, he emphasized that the choice was about seeing if he could reach his full potential. This drive to become the best version of themselves is at the heart of what makes the GOATs so special.

The problem with the word *mastery* is that it doesn't tell you much about what it takes to get there. It sounds good to try and become the best version of yourself, but *how* do you actually do that? What are the skills you need to truly excel and become the best that you can be?

The ability to be our best when it counts is about control. It's about not being taken off our game by a bad play or by the taunts of an opponent. Rather, it's about remaining positive and confident when a technology blip takes a presentation sideways. It's about staying objective and controlling our emotions when something really serious happens. All of us are depended upon by family, friends, coworkers, and even strangers to remain cool and collected when adversity strikes. When our performance is on the line, we need to control our emotions to be at our best.

For us to reach our full potential, the science is clear: one psychological skill stands above the rest—self-regulation. As a coach of professional athletes, I can personally attest to self-regulation as a necessary skill to perform well and live well. Self-regulation is the ability to direct our thoughts, emotions, and behaviors in order to achieve our goals (called "self-mastery"). It is the fifth in our set of psychological skills (or qualities of performance) and builds on the four you have learned about so far: capacity, mental strength, endurance, and flexibility.

Our ability to self-regulate is at the center of what separates the best from the rest. At the highest levels of professional soccer, for example, those highest in self-regulation are likely to make more national team appearances (a sign that they've risen to maximal heights) and to perform better than their less well-regulated professional peers.[1,2] In academic settings, those higher in self-regulation get better grades.[3] In an operating room, surgeons high in self-regulation achieve better outcomes.[4,5]

The ability to self-regulate and optimize our own learning has led to the development of some of the greatest talents across sports. Roger Federer talks about setting goals in simple terms so he can reflect, question those goals, and make adjustments to the nature of the goal or the timeframe (the hallmarks of self-regulated learning). Lewis Hamilton talks about mastering his emotions to master the car (the hallmarks of self-mastery). Kobe Bryant was famous for his "Mamba Mentality," the ability to be present and rigorous in his execution. For each of these athletes, the core of their excellence stems back to their ability to get their brain and body exactly where they need for performance. Anywhere you find greatness, you'll find self-regulation.

SELF-REGULATION, PART 1: SELF-MASTERY

If self-mastery is about control, what are the things we can reasonably try and control to facilitate peak performance? You'll often hear sport psychologists talk about "controlling the controllables." What that really means is being able to control and direct your thoughts (like your attitude or positivity), emotions (like your intensity of anger, joy, or passion), physiology (like your heart rate, breathing, and energy), and behavior (like your effort and persistence) in a way that enhances your performance.

Thinking, Feeling, and Physiology

What does it mean to be able to control and direct our thoughts, emotions, physiology and, ultimately, our behavior? You might be thinking something like having discipline and being able to control our emotions. More than this, though, high performers are able to optimize the way they use their thoughts and emotions to facilitate their performance. They see stress as adaptive, have a wide range of strategies for dealing with feelings, and leverage several tactics to make their inner voice a performance coach. It's not just about being disciplined and consistent, or stoic in the way we experience our emotions. It's about knowing our inner experience so much that we can use it to determine what we need to rise to the top.

It's the highest form of self-management. For top performers, this level of awareness and control allows them to deploy the right skill at the right time to keep themselves in their optimal zone of functioning. This means dealing with unexpected challenges and adapting to stay on task or course. Self-regulation skills allow us to efficiently and dynamically realign around the most energy efficient way to complete a task. Balance is restored and we continue working toward our goals.

With a high degree of control and direction over how we think, feel and behave, we can start to express the highest and best versions of ourselves. In a fascinating line of research, the foundations of "sporting genius" boil down to knowing what skills to use in what context (self-mastery), paired with self-belief (a source of confidence and courage); creativity (being innovative, such as changing an approach or tactic in the moment); and risk-taking (the drive to achieve the high and hard goal).[6] A lack of confidence, poor thinking, and avoiding risk are all barriers to real excellence.

Our thoughts, feelings, and physiology are intertwined and directly impact our behavior. Now, when I say "control" and "direct," I don't mean literally "control" as in being able to specifically dictate exactly what you think or feel (though the highest performers do in fact control the thoughts they have, by learning to defuse from unhelpful thoughts and to generate the thoughts they need to act impactfully). Most of our thinking and feeling happens automatically, without our conscious awareness. Control means to be able to change, shift, adapt, or adjust our thinking and feeling to best serve our goals. So, what can we do to better direct thinking and feeling and physiology over the long term? Diana Taurasi provides us with a great example.

Coach's Corner: Readiness and Regulation

Diana Taurasi's pre-game routine in the WNBA highlights the direct link between good preparation and good self-regulation. She can walk you through *exactly* how she wants to feel thirty minutes before the game starts, then ten minutes before the game starts, and at tipoff. Calm and focused, then ramped up, and then at peace. And she learned to get into that state by learning to self-regulate.

The better we prepare, the more in control of our performance we are. The more in control we are, the better we are at self-regulating. It's another virtuous performance cycle, in which practicing self-regulation leads to better preparation, better performance, and the ability to regulate, again and again.

Context Sensitivity, Repertoire, and Feedback

Having control of your thoughts, emotions, physiology, and behavior is facilitated by the three critical factors we'll explore below. Each of these factors helps us to determine the *right* action in the present moment, which is critical to top performance. The best performers know what skill to use in what context and are able to deploy that skill on command to deliver when it matters most.

Context Sensitivity

The first of the three factors is what psychologists call *context sensitivity*. Context sensitivity is essentially how tuned in we are to the environment, and what the environment says is a necessary response at this moment. The environment is where your attention should be when you're performing. Paying attention to what's happening in the moment allows you to figure out what action is needed next. And, as a bonus, tuning into the environment facilitates *flow*, an optimal psychological experience that tends to lead to peak performance.[7]

Imagine, for example, that you're a firefighter responding to a home engulfed in flames with family members inside. As soon as you get the call, your body will experience a cascade of physiological and neurochemical changes. Your cortisol and adrenaline will increase, and your brain will start to anticipate the challenge ahead. Regardless of how many times you've responded to a scenario like this (some firefighters have hundreds of reps under their belts), the same basic changes will occur.

If you weren't so sensitive to the environment, your performance would suffer. You've heard the saying, "When you're a hammer, everything looks like a nail." When you're low in context sensitivity, everything looks like a cookie-cutter situation. Each house fire begins to look the same, and this state causes you to miss important details, like the safest way to enter *this* home. This could lead to making mistakes and failing to put the fire out in the shortest time possible and, tragically, loss of life. On top of that, when the fire is out, you'd have a hard time coming down and recovering again. Your brain and body would still be in mission mode, pumping unnecessary energy hormones to galvanize a response that's no longer needed. On the next go-round, you'd likely be energy deficient. Unfortunately, that's a recipe for the start of a vicious cycle, in which you take mental shortcuts the next time around, again failing to detect critical details for success.

Now let's assume you've got the right calibration to your environment. You arrive on the scene and immediately your brain starts to adapt. Your brain and body should experience a fine-tuning of the stress response and of your neurochemistry, adapted to the current situation based on your extensive training. You've likely seen something similar before. Your brain and body, with high context sensitivity, can now project more accurately what will be needed to successfully douse the fire and rescue the family members still inside the home.

Context sensitivity helps us ramp up or ramp down quickly and effectively based on what we're experiencing. Suppose given your extensive training, you find a quick resolution to the fire and a safe way to extract the family. Once your mission is complete, the context has changed again—there's no need to be so energized. Instead, you can shift to rest and recovery to adequately prepare for the next situation. People high in context sensitivity can detect those changes that are significant and, as a result, are able to redirect their thinking, feeling, and physiology back to an appropriate level.

A Broad Repertoire of Behaviors

The second feature of effective regulation is a broad *repertoire* of behaviors. Your repertoire refers to the range of skills you have available to deploy in any situation, including both in a high-performance context and in everyday life. After reading this book, your repertoire should include a range of things you can do to help yourself think, feel, and perform better.

Let's go back to you as a firefighter for a moment. If you have the right range of skills, you know how to adequately prepare. You've done mental and physical practice and are ready to perform. You also know how to regulate your energy efficiency; you can ramp up or down using your breathing, focal cues, and grounding techniques. You've trained your mind to be present, letting go of distracting thoughts like "What will happen if we don't get to the people in time?" and instead focusing on what you can control, right here and now. Because you're fully present, you can make quick and accurate decisions, smoothly executing the mission. And if you hit a setback, you know how to release that mistake, reset, and refocus so that you can respond resiliently and finish the job.

In essence, this is about being a Leatherman instead of a hammer. A Leatherman multi-tool offers up to fifty or more tools and is capable of performing a wide range of tasks. With a broad repertoire of behaviors, you can decide when to hammer and when something else might be better, which makes you more adaptable and increases your performative fit with the environment.

Feedback

The final element of effective regulation is *feedback*. Feedback plays a critical role in our ability to change and adapt our behavior. Feedback can come from several sources, including the environment, ourselves, and the people around us.

The first—the environment—is an important data point for performers to constantly monitor. Think back to the burning home. Imagine that you start to hear the crackling associated with higher-intensity flames. That data—feedback from the environment—will influence what course of action to take. You need to be able to adjust on the fly, either expediting your extraction of the people inside or choosing an alternate route to get to them. Without tuning into that environmental feedback, you're liable to make a mistake.

Feedback from the people around you is also critical. For the firefighters on the scene, clear communication and feedback from teammates is essential. You'd want to know if your teammate spotted something critical to the mission, like something falling behind you as you enter the home. This feedback allows you to determine that you need a new path out, without having to assess for yourself. You can adjust your behavior, reduce the time spent analyzing, and give yourself a better chance of success.

You also want to pay attention to the feedback coming from within. People often think of this as their "gut instinct," but data show that for high performers, that gut instinct is really expert judgment.[8] You want to take your gut instinct seriously. If you're feeling more nervous than normal, it might be a sign that you're missing an important piece of data. If you're calmer than anticipated, it might be a sign that your brain or body isn't fully ready for performance. Each of these data points is feedback for you to enhance your performance.

SELF-REGULATION, PART 2: SELF-REGULATED LEARNING

An important aspect of what separates high performers from average performers is the quality of reflection on the skills being mastered. The best in the world are all, first and foremost, *experts*. And self-regulated learning is all about developing that expertise so that you can demonstrate to the world what's possible when the lights come on.

On the pitch, ice rink, or court, you have an opportunity to perform according to the skills you've developed through hard work, practice, and play. You are able to measure progress over time. The scoreboard, to a degree, reflects the practice you've put in and the skills you've mastered, what you've learned, and what you have left to do.

Achieving our potential is a result of putting in the time and effort to learn. Without learning, there's no progress. The better we can learn and the more efficient we can get with our regular practice and deployment of skills, the better we can perform. This is the road to mastery.

The best learning takes place in practice. This is the time for you to try new things, to take risks, to push yourself without fear of failure. When you engage in practice like that, you encourage deeper development. Your performance in practice might suffer, but who cares? The path to optimal learning is paved with failures. Each of them makes you a little wiser and better, pushing you closer to the top of your potential.

Realizing our potential to one day hit our peak also requires an ongoing exploration of our passions and interests. This wide-ranging exploration allows for creative insights and synthesis, which push us forward in our thinking and action. In the true spirit of expertise, this forward momentum only highlights what we don't know, and the cycle of exploration continues. The more we learn, the more we see how much further we have to go.

The Three Phases of Self-Regulated Learning

Self-regulated learning follows an iterative cycle consisting of three phases. In the first phase, we set a goal and develop a plan. What is it that we're working toward, and how do we want to get there? What's the best path to take? The goal and the plan create a context for us to develop our skills and give us something clear to focus on when we get to practice or performance.

Take, for example, the NBA player who wants to get better at shooting. Improving shooting is a big, important, but vague goal. To really learn to improve your shooting, you need to break it down into smaller goals (improve your footwork) and have a plan for doing so (work closely with a coach who gives constant feedback about your footwork). Without those two ingredients, the player is likely to resort to ineffective tactics to develop, like simply going to the gym every night of the week and shooting hoops. The more focused, self-regulated learner will take fewer shots or even the same number of shots, but with a higher quality as a function of how focused they are on the objective they have set.

The second phase is about active monitoring and adjusting, meaning that as you work your plan to reach your goal, you keep track of what's going on. Are you getting closer or further away? Is what you're doing working? As you go, you answer these questions and make small adjustments to maximize the value of the practice.

Let's get back to our NBA player. In the case of improving footwork, they're consciously monitoring their footwork—location, speed, and placement, for example—rather than focusing on hitting the three-pointer. In this case, the mark of a good shot isn't a made basket but mastering the right footwork to make a shot consistently. At each rep, the athlete is consciously noting what's working and what needs adjustment. This allows them to make important changes in real time and to get the most out of the reps they take.

The final phase is to reflect and adjust. Did today's work get you closer to your goal? Is the plan still correct? What else needs to happen? If you can answer these questions effectively, you set yourself up for a great chance to get better again tomorrow.

In my work with NBA athletes, I teach them a simple, three-step process for reflection. I ask them to answer the same questions each day:

1. What did you do today that you want to keep doing?

2. What did you do today that you want to do differently?

3. What did you learn?

You'll notice these questions are designed to be observational and non-judgmental in tone. This isn't about your evaluation of what you did

> well or poorly, but of what behavior you want to iterate on. Self-regulated learning is the process of becoming a scientist about your own performance. If you can do that, you can rapidly develop your expertise.

TIGER WOODS: A MASTER OF SELF-MASTERY

We see self-regulation play out in live time in the most historic moments in sports. It's the clutch shot at the buzzer from Michael Jordan or the long putt from Tiger in his Sunday red. It's the calm service of match point before the emotional collapse to the knees in Wimbledon, and the game-winning touchdown drive led by a composed quarterback.

Imagine the self-mastery and expertise required to sink a chip shot from the rough in golf. You're faced with the task of getting out of a precarious position before you can even think about making the shot. But when an elite performer like Tiger Woods approaches a shot like this, all of his self-regulation abilities shine through clearly.

It was the 2005 Masters, the 16th hole on the last day. His standing in the tournament hanging in the balance. The shot I just described is tough, but now imagine it under the pressure of winning it all. Miss this shot, and he'd have no chance of taking home the green jacket.

How does the best golfer in the world approach something like that? First, he started by inspecting the green. He came up with a clear plan and strategy to reach his goal (make the shot). Once the decision was made, based on his years of experience, it was time to put the plan into action.

Before he stepped up to swing, he went through his routine, designed to help him stay calm and focused under pressure. He uses the technique of staying present to help him manage the pressure, famously telling his son, "The next shot should be the most important shot in your life. It should be more important than breathing." This level of commitment to the here and now, and the task at hand, helps guide his attention away from unhelpful thoughts and to the only thing that matters—making the shot.

As he followed through and watched the ball travel through the air, the tournament hung in the balance. The ball ended up hanging on the lip of a hole for a brief moment … until the final rotation nudged it in. Tiger went on to win the tournament. This level of self-regulation—to know exactly what he needed from himself to make one of the most difficult shots in the game—is what separates the best from the rest.

* * *

Self-mastery and self-regulated learning are the hallmarks of elite performers, and the foundational practices that go into each of them are simple but not easy. My coaching practice is built on qualities and principles of performance that create the conditions to build these two skills.

In the first part of the book, you've learned about the skills you need to develop self-mastery and expertise over the long term. We've covered what it means to be flexible and mentally strong, and how to build your adaptive capacity so that you can continue to improve over time. You've learned about mindsets you can embrace about stress and different ways to manage your thoughts or feelings in service of your values. Each of these tools is designed to help you have greater control over yourself, so that you can consistently move toward becoming the best you can be.

As we move into part two, you'll see how self-regulation separates the best from the rest when the lights are brightest. Under pressure, you must be able to use your energy effectively, to stay focused and present, and to bounce back from setbacks. Each of these requires learning: about the game or performance, about yourself, and about what you need to succeed. They also require self-mastery and the ability to not get too rattled as the intensity rises. All of this starts with what you'll learn next about preparation, the first of five principles which collectively create the foundation for peak performance. What do you need to master before the game even begins? See you in part two.

ENDNOTES

1. Tynke Toering, MarijeT. Elferink-Gemser, Geir Jordet, and Chris Visscher, "Self-Regulation and Performance Level of Elite and Non-Elite Youth Soccer Players." *Journal of Sports Sciences* 27(14) (2009): 1509-1517. https://doi.org/10.1080/02640410903369919.

2. Tynke Toering, MarijeT. Elferink-Gemser, Geir Jordet, Gert-Jan Pepping, and Chris Visscher, "Self-Regulation of Learning and Performance Level of Elite Youth Soccer Players." *International Journal of Sport Psychology* 43(4) (2012): 312-325.

3. Laura Nota, Salvatore Soresi, and Barry J. Zimmerman, "Self-Regulation and Academic Achievement and Resilience: A Longitudinal Study." *International Journal of Educational Research* 41(3) (2004): 198-215. https://doi.org/10.1016/j.ijer.2005.07.001.

4. Michael Inzlicht, Kaitlyn M. Werner, Julia L. Briskin, and Brent W. Roberts, "Integrating Models of Self-Regulation." *Annual Review of Psychology* 72(1) (2021): 319-345. https://doi.org/10.1146/annurev-psych-061020-105721.

5. Anya L. Greenberg et al., "Emotional Regulation in Surgery: Fostering Well-Being, Performance, and Leadership." *Journal of Surgical Research* 277 (2022): A25-A35. https://doi.org/10.1016/jss.2022.02.032.

6. Joe Higgins, "Why Roger Federer Is a GOAT: An Account of Sporting Genius." *Journal of the Philosophy of Sport* 45(3) (2018): 296-317. https://doi.org/10.1080/00948705.2018.1520126.

7. Mihaly Csikszentmihalyi, *Flow and the Foundations of Positive Psychology: The Collected Works of Mihaly Csikszentmihalyi* (2014): 227-238. https://doi.org/10.1007/978-94-017-9088-8.

8. Daniel Kahneman and Gary Klein, "Conditions for Intuitive Expertise: A Failure to Disagree." *American Psychologist* 64(6) (2009): 515.

PART 2:

THE PRINCIPLES OF PEAK PERFORMANCE

INTRODUCTION

I joined the Toronto Raptors in March of 2020, just eleven days before the world was shut down by the COVID-19 pandemic, and about seven months after the team had raised a championship trophy as the best franchise in the league. My onboarding into the role was a full immersion into managing the uncertainty of a global pandemic for a group of high performers who had recently fulfilled a lifelong dream and were preparing to do it again. As it became clear that we weren't going to be playing any basketball for a few months, I was presented with a unique opportunity. I had the chance to actually reflect with the players on what allowed them to win the championship, and to then try and do my part to support them on that journey again.

What I uncovered as I got to know the players was remarkable. Most of them could remember where they sat during the games, the role they played, how many points they scored, places they faltered, and the moment it became certain they were about to be world champions. This experience had changed not only the way they understood the game of basketball, but also how they understood themselves. This massive moment redefined their careers, forever. They were no longer just NBA players, but world champions. This one series changed them. And most of them had some idea about what they needed to do to deliver that peak performance again.

But what I observed that was most notable, as a new person joining the organization, was that their winning a championship wasn't just about the trophy. It was a total transformation.

That's the real impact of a peak performance.

We're wired to remember the big moments. There's a blend of emotion, immediate feedback, competence, connectedness, and progress—the signatures of flow—that make these moments so memorable. These are the moments you play for, that define you, that pave the path to your own championship.

Peak performance is that perfect pitch you delivered to a prospective new client or the game-winning strike you threw. No matter what your performance arena, there are times that require us to be our best when it matters most. Though replicating an elite performance in a sport, like Kobe Bryant's eighty-point game, is well out of reach for most of us, the psychological state he was in to deliver such a memorable performance is squarely within our control. You can deliver an eighty-point game in your arena, consistently, with practice and a few other tools you'll be introduced to in the coming chapters.

What we humans take for granted is that you can *optimize* for peak performance, no matter what your performance is. The way we optimize is by first identifying how we currently show up to performance, and then identifying how we want to show up for performance and what skills we need to bridge that gap. This is the chasm we need to cross to elevate our game. Thankfully, there is a set of skills you can learn and choose from that can help you find your way.

But bear this in mind: While the skills themselves are important, an overemphasis on honing mental skills has led people to believe that the best way to reach peak performance is some formulaic application of traditional sport psychology skills, such as goal-setting or arousal regulation. To be clear, these skills matter, but they don't come anywhere close to being a blueprint for great performance, and they certainly won't be the skills everyone needs to get to peak performance. I've worked with plenty of top athletes who couldn't clearly articulate their goals, and conversely with others who were able to clearly state their goals and milestones. I've worked with athletes who are over-aroused and channel their energy in the moment when it matters most, and others who wake up from a nap (in other words, are in a low-arousal state) until right before the lights come on.

I'll also discuss the states I've found to be correlated to high performance. These states are the athlete's barometer. They routinely ask themselves things, such as "How will I respond to adversity? Do I have the right amount of excitement and energy? Am I well prepared?" By entering the conversation at the level of performance states, performers are not limited to searching for a narrow skill set. I do not coach within a narrow, rigid application of a canon of skills. The idea is to access a set of psychological states that create a context for peak performance to emerge.

If you want to learn how to show up for the moments that matter most in life, the five principles provide the answer key. We'll begin by exploring the steps for excellent preparation, which is the starting point for any great performance. We'll then explore the four psychological states athletes engage to perform relentlessly at their best, and how you can engage those same four states for yourself. Along the way, you'll be introduced to skills you can try and apply and ideas that can elevate your game. Let's get started.

PRINCIPLE #1:

Preparation

Free-soloing makes up only a small percentage of my total climbing. But when I do solo, I manage the risk through careful preparation.

– Alex Honnold

El Capitan is a 3,000-foot behemoth rock face in Yosemite Valley. It represents one of the most formidable of challenges that top climbers can take on. Each year in Yosemite, over one hundred climbers are injured while attempting to scale the face of the mountain. Over thirty people have died in an attempt. Summiting El Capitan places a climber at the pinnacle of performance, both literally and figuratively. It's one of the most challenging feats of human performance.

Performances like summiting a mountain are truly matters of life and death. In such instances, a wrong move, a miscalculated step, or an unaccounted-for condition can be the difference between a successful ascent and an injury (or worse). *And Alex Honnold sets out to do it without a rope.*

In the acclaimed documentary *Free Solo*, the viewer is granted the privilege of an intimate portrait of Honnold's meticulous preparation to summit El Capitan. We get to witness how he manages adversity in his response to injuries. We see how he manages his relationships with loved ones who are acutely aware of the level of risk involved. He gives us a remarkably accurate picture of the unique demands and challenges of exceptional performance.

The documentary begins with Honnold framing the challenge and what it means to climb El Capitan. The viewer is introduced to his colleagues and friends who have either attempted the summit themselves and failed, have completed the summit with a rope, or are intimately connected to those members of the climbing community who lost their lives in an attempt to reach the peak.

THE SECRET SAUCE OF HONNOLD'S TRAINING REGIMEN: PREPARATION

Interspersed throughout the scenes of the mountain and stories of climbers, we are given glimpses into Honnold's regimen for preparing for the ascent: pull-ups from the frame of his car; journaling the moves that he makes in practice; and reflecting on what has worked, what needs to be different, and what he has learned and needs to learn (more on that later in the chapter).

Between breathtaking images of the mountain itself, the arc of the story of Honnold's romantic relationship, and the stories of his colleagues recounting his climbing acumen, it's easy to take for granted one of the hidden yet most important parts of this story: Preparation for performance like this is *simple* (but not easy).

What separates Alex from the rest of the climbers is not his unique neural circuitry, unparalleled physical capabilities, or an unrivaled fearlessness, though there's some evidence he possesses all three of these as a function of his level of training. Rather, it's his meticulous, detailed, and thorough approach to preparing. By the time he gets to the climb itself, execution is almost second nature. He's separated himself not through some form of mysticism, but from a simple ability to engage in the task of preparation *repeatedly*, almost ad nauseam, to reflect on the repetition, refine it with *variation*, and make the training *representative* of the climb itself. Though the viewer is kept on the edge of their seats, we intuitively anticipate Honnold's success—and not because we know how the film ends. It's because, almost subconsciously, we've absorbed just how hard he's worked in preparing for this performance. Given his attention to detail and commitment to training, it's almost impossible to imagine another outcome.

Great performance, done right, is simple. That's not the same as easy. Simple, in this instance, is a reference to the tendency to overcomplicate success as we get progressively higher up the mountain. The higher the level of performance, the more we tend to think that there is some ethereal skill set or tactical plan that separates the best from the rest. What Alex Honnold teaches us is that the preparation for the climb itself has no frills, no special secrets or mystical practices—just simple, steady practice and psychological preparation. Though he undoubtedly is physically gifted and possesses great mental fortitude, he illustrates that these are skills which can be trained.

As we see his progress unfold, we're given front-row seats to the readiness formula from one of the world's best: **readiness = practice x psychological preparation.** This is the foundational equation of his skill development and indeed may be his superpower. Honnold's superpower can be developed by anyone wanting and willing to train for peak performance, and for most of us under far less demanding conditions.

He masterfully illustrates his developing readiness throughout the documentary. As the film unfolds, we see Honnold's lifestyle in anticipation of the climb, the steps he takes to manage his fear, and the dynamic, varied, purposeful practice he engages in. He knows that a successful summit involves maximizing his readiness by minimizing the consequences of an adverse event, whether it is a psychological challenge because the climb is delayed due to poor weather or missing a foothold and having to stabilize his balance.

He studies a specific part of the mountain face to come to know it intimately. He spends hours calculating the same moves over and over again, testing the limits of what he's capable of and assessing his execution. He makes notes and strategizes and consults with colleagues. He strength trains. He spends time practicing on the mountain.

Yet the physical preparation is only half the battle. As Honnold and the other climbers constantly point out, the other aspect of a successful climb is mental. It's about managing fear. On the Tim Ferris podcast, Honnold recounts how he prepares for such a climb using a skill we will visit shortly: mental rehearsal: "Particularly if it's a free solo, I'm climbing ropeless, then I'll think through what it'll feel like to be in certain positions, because some kinds of movements are insecure and so they're kind of scarier than other types of moves, and so it's important to me think through how that'll feel when I'm up there, so that when I'm doing it I don't suddenly be like, 'Oh my God, this is really scary!' I know that it's supposed to be scary; I know that's going to be the move; I know what it'll feel like, and I just do it." He's managing his fear not by running from it or acting like it isn't real, but from proactively engaging with it.

Here Honnold is again, this time more explicitly on managing the (appropriate) fear: "I'm not trying to control the fear exactly. I try to **prepare** to the point where I'm not feeling afraid. ... It is not as if I take something very scary and suppress that fear and just do it anyway. I take something scary and identify the reasons why it is scary. ... I work through those things, and eventually I do it when it doesn't feel scary anymore." He trains so that neither his physical training nor his mental training limits his performance.

While very few human beings are capable of summiting a rock face without a rope, for the rest of us mere mortals the point is that practice and psychological preparation can help all of us summit our own El Cap. The more you do of both, the more ready you will be. If you focus on one at the expense of the other, you fail to optimize the odds that you'll reach your goal. Just like Alex Honnold, high performers work until their physical and mental abilities don't hold them back.

| THE SCIENCE OF PREPARING WELL

All performances are odds-based events. What that means is, no matter how good you are at what you do, there will always be factors beyond your control that will influence the ultimate outcome. In the case of summiting El Cap, it might be a sudden onset of bad weather. In the NBA, it might be a flight delay that has the potential to compromise the team's performance come game time. In parenting, it might be an unexpected illness of your partner that leaves you needing to pick up the slack. The good news, however, is that there are several factors well within your control that can give you the best chance of success. That best chance starts with *readiness*. If performance is an odds-based event, readiness is how we stack the odds in our favor.

Let me restate the formula: readiness is a combination of practice and psychological preparation. While either one in isolation can help you to feel more ready to take on a challenge, the combination of the two gives you the best chance for your best performance because they address the most critical dimensions of execution: efficient execution of our skill (be it a presentation, a golf swing, or a sales pitch), anticipating challenges and how to deal with them (internal and external—but more on that shortly), and putting our body and mind in our optimal state.

Purposeful Practice

Practice can be either purposeful or pointless. In theory, practice should be developing the skill necessary to execute during a pressure-packed moment. At a basic level, practice is about what sport psychologists call *automaticity*. Automaticity is the idea that we can rehearse a specific skill to the point that it becomes, quite literally, automatic. In a technical sense, automaticity means that we've rehearsed a particular skill so much that our brain and body can execute that skill with optimal energy efficiency. Execution, then, becomes easier with practice.

I am going to introduce two types of practice that lead to automatic execution and help us perform our best in dynamic conditions: purposeful practice and deliberate practice. While they sound similar, the two concepts are different, and in in very important ways. **Purposeful practice** combines three elements of effective skill-building: *repetition, variation,* and *representativeness*. **Deliberate practice** refers to a very specific type of practice dedicated to skill-building and it consists of four factors, which I discuss below.[1]

Repetition—and Why It's Not Quite Enough

Purposeful practice stands in direct contrast to the type of practice most of us were exposed to as kids. When you're first starting a sport, you take the same shot over and again. When you're memorizing your sales pitch, you simply repeat it over and over until you have it down. When you wanted to ace a test, chances are you simply tried to memorize facts until you learned

PRINCIPLE #1: Preparation

more sophisticated techniques, like using notecards or paraphrasing your reading. You were taught that repetition leads to execution. This rote exercise is only a beginning. It's not a standalone methodology. It can't prepare us for the dynamic nature of most performances. After all, NBA players rarely shoot without an opponent trying to block the shot. Pitches to investors aren't given in an empty room.

Rote practice is inadequate for several reasons, but the primary reason lies in the mismatch between rote practice and the demands of performance. There are almost no performances where we will get to execute a skill entirely without distraction. How many times have you seen a quarterback throw a pass with no defensive linemen bearing down on them? How many account managers are able to give perhaps the biggest sales pitch of their career to clients who are ready to buy, no questions asked?

Rote exercise can work for getting a pass to the flat or a sales deck down pat, but it won't come close to maximizing your practice potential. The reason this strategy is limited is that there's minimal *transfer* between the rote practice and the context of the performance itself. The two are (largely) uncorrelated. Rote practice won't prepare you for novel situations, like a wet ball on the gridiron or a hostile member of the audience in a conference hall. This problem of transfer is part of why psychologists suggest preparing for a test in the same room you're going to take it in (what's called "state-dependent learning"). Preparing for the test in the same room where you'll be taking the test is a (small) step in the direction of the context of the performance itself.

For practice to really work, we have to make it as lifelike as possible, assuming that we have the fundamentals of our performance down. Practicing in front of an empty room will help you become marginally better the first few times, but it won't position you to perform at your best when the room fills up and you're challenged with questions in real time. You need some repetition, but repetition alone is not enough.

Variation

Variation is about changing the context and circumstances in which we rehearse a specific skill for performance. In anticipation of the varying conditions of our performance, we should practice under varying conditions. For example, if we're preparing for a musical, it might help to start with an empty auditorium, to gradually introduce audience members, and then to practice in front of a full house (there's a reason we have dress rehearsals, after all). A golfer who never plays in inclement weather will be unprepared for and unequal to rain and wind. To get even more out of it, the best performers will experiment widely. They'll practice while tired, in bad weather, or in new surroundings. The goal isn't to account for *every* possibility; the goal is to introduce enough variation in practice conditions so that unanticipated conditions that arise during performance won't disrupt the effortless execution they've worked so hard to master.

Though it's become a bit of a meme, Steph Curry's warm-up shooting is an exercise in variation and how it leads to expertise. If you've watched any NBA highlights in the past few years, you've seen Steph shooting the ball—and not just on the court. He's hit shots from the second set of stands in the arena, from behind the backboard, and even from the opening of the tunnel where the teams run onto the court.

Pre-game, this routine serves several purposes for Steph, and it neatly illustrates how variation can lead to expert performance. He's able to make these shots because he's practiced shooting under a variety of conditions, and these shots are extensions of that variation.

The beauty of this exercise is that after tip-off you get to watch him sink threes from all over the court because the variation in practice has created a rich mental model to draw on to execute. The variation in his practice makes shooting with a hand in his face as seamless as an open shot, and a half-court shot as effortless as a layup.

Representativeness

The third element of purposeful practice is representativeness, which simply means that parts of practice mimic the conditions of the game. Where variation is about trying the skill under varying conditions, representativeness is about trying to perform the skill as close to the performance as possible. This is why scrimmaging is valuable and why teams across all sports engage in pre-season play. The closer we can get to practice replicating the real conditions of performance, the better our performance will be.

Representativeness maximizes the odds of the skill transfer we talked about earlier. It's why there's no replacement for real reps. When you look at Alex Honnold's preparation for El Capitan, his practice was highly representative—each repetition and each practice he did was on the mountain and on the route he was likely to take and under the actual conditions he might experience.

The greater the representation, the greater the likelihood the skill will show up when we need it most. And there are more opportunities for representative practice than we typically think.

An entrepreneur I'll call John is a pre-seed start-up founder who is raising money for a training program he's built that uses data to assess and build leadership competencies. He came to me about two weeks before a series of pitches he had to investors in what's colloquially called a "road show," wherein he'd visit a handful of investors in several major cities in order to quickly raise capital. And he called me because, for the first time in his life, he was nervous about speaking in public.

Nerves like this aren't uncommon in the context of big performances. After all, this road show was going to determine whether or not he'd get to continue pursuing his dream. As we started to uncover some of the reasons for these nerves, one thing became clear: he hadn't practiced enough under the right conditions to have a real sense of what it would *feel* like to pitch to these investors. He had the lines memorized, but it's one thing to recite them in the shower and quite another when you have to deliver them with a high level of controlled energy to a group of people who might write a million-dollar check.

So, in addition to the arousal-management strategies we used together, which you'll learn about shortly, we set out to get John some more representative practice. We started with small audiences, like his family and friends, and worked our way up to larger audiences. He even gave the pitch over a grocery store microphone. Then the day came when we were able to get him some scheduled pitches with investors who weren't part of the road show but might nevertheless write a check.

The experience culminated with a pitch day in front of some of the US's biggest investors on a sunny, humid day in Austin, Texas. John had five minutes to give his pitch along with nine other entrepreneurs also looking for investment. He had essentially five minutes to prove himself and his product as worthy of investment.

When he recounted the story of the pitch to me, he said, "For about the first thirty seconds, my mind was a little blank. I started to worry I wouldn't be able to execute. And I just reminded myself to simply say the first line. Once I got that first line out, I realized this was just another rep. This was the same pitch I've now given a hundred times, to people just like this. And then I hit flow, and it went off without a hitch."

John's representative practice enabled him to deliver his best when it mattered most. He left the pitch day with enough funding to keep the company afloat for another eighteen months, and with a new sense of mastery over his ability to communicate the value and vision for his company.

Deliberate Practice

The term *deliberate practice* was coined by psychologist Anders Ericsson.[2] It refers to a very specific type of practice dedicated to skill-building in pursuit of expertise. It consists of four factors: (1) a focus on a specific goal, (2) a focus on improvement, (3) receiving immediate feedback, and (4) getting out of our comfort zone. In his research, Dr. Ericsson determined that deliberate practice is a necessary requisite for becoming an expert.

The first component, a focus on a specific goal, means placing the target of our practice at the forefront of our mind in a concrete, specific way. The average performer shows up to practice with the idea that they just want to "get better," based on the assumption that more hours, no matter the quality, will lead to better performance. The high performer, on the other hand, understands that having a specific focus for their practice regimen will enable them to reduce their performance gaps by identifying weaknesses and mitigating them, and developing the specific skills necessary to deliver under pressure. Consequently, the highest performers have higher-quality practice in less time. Over time, this narrow focus on a specific target leads to big improvements, which is the second element of deliberate practice.

For us to really know if practice is working, we need immediate feedback. Psychologists have demonstrated time and again that feedback close to the execution of a behavior is the most impactful, and feedback about practice is no different. Immediate feedback is the gateway to figuring out what to modify between repetitions. Feedback is like a laser beam focusing on improvement—it guides our attention and shines a light on what we can continue working on. Without it, we practice in the dark, with no clear direction on if we are performing the skill at the efficiency we need, and what to change to keep improving if we are not.

For deliberate practice to be effective, then, you need to take this feedback and adjust accordingly. That doesn't mean that you must accept and apply *all* feedback, but only quality feedback that can guide improve your focus to help you improve. If you can stay focused on getting better, consistently, each time you practice, you're likely to develop the expertise you need to be your best when it matters most.

Coach's Corner: Providing Effective Feedback

There's a science to delivering good feedback.[3] Good feedback is:

- **Timely.** If too much time passes between the action and the feedback, it's harder for the learner to connect the dots. You want your feedback to land as close to the performance as possible, so your team member can see the clear link between what they've done and what you're asking of them.

- **Clear.** Good feedback should be easy to understand and apply. Often, that means it's focused on one thing, and that's it. You have to resist the tendency to address multiple things at once, and instead clearly communicate suggestions to work on one change.

- **Personally relevant.** This may seem obvious, but the person receiving the feedback has to feel it applies to them for it to work. If you give feedback and someone isn't changing, chances are they don't see the feedback as relevant enough to them to change.

- **Given frequently.** There's a trope in sales that customers must hear something eight to ten times before they buy. The same is true for feedback. Your subject needs to hear it often for the feedback to stick.

- **Positive and constructive.** The best feedback gives people something to *do* differently and helps them focus on *how to succeed versus how to not fail.*

Finally, deliberate practice should get us out of our comfort zones. Top performers know that growth happens just past the edge of what we think we are capable of. It also happens to be where flow, or that sense that we are perfectly "in the zone," can occur. Research has confirmed that practicing skills just beyond our comfort zone—what's been termed as a "desirable difficulty"—ultimately improves long-term skill retention and performance.[4]

These desirable difficulties lead to performers using deeper learning strategies, which enable them to more fluently retrieve the relevant skill in multiple contexts (kind of like what we try to do with varying practice). Practicing at the edge will ultimately let you perform at the edge.

Pushing beyond what is comfortable enables us to execute when it matters most. During practice, our performance should not be flawless. If it is, it's a sign that we are not practicing as hard as we should be. As a coach, I remedy this by aiming for higher, harder goals, and running small experiments with new behaviors. Anytime you're working on developing a skill, you should actually experience a slight *dip* in performance as you search for what's right from a handful of options.[5] Only once you've identified what's right should you have a *leap* forward that leads you to a higher level of mastery.

Even if we feel we are adequately practiced for the skill we need to perform, practice becomes a way to take ourselves to the next level and over-deliver when it counts. The goal is for the practice to be harder than the performance, so that when we arrive to the performance we've already worked through elements considerably more challenging than those we are about to face. Some of the greatest athletes of all time, like Tom Brady, reiterate this same principle as a key part of their preparation. They push themselves hard in practice so that the performance is *easier* than a typical day at the office.

With deliberate practice and the right practice under dynamic conditions, we should be moving progressively closer to our performance mastery, or what the experts call "automaticity": a sense of automatic, effortless execution.[6] Effective practice in this way is half of the readiness equation. We put ourselves in a position to execute, and, if we can effectively manage the psychological aspects of preparation and performance, we increase our odds of a top performance even more.

With adequate practice one of the biggest challenges to peak performance can be taken off the table. But another challenge remains, and it is found within ourselves. It is rooted in the fear of failure.

Psychological Preparation

Assuming we've practiced to the point that the execution is as seamless as can be, much of performance becomes about making sure we don't inadvertently self-defeat our drive for excellence. We do this through psychological preparation where we *build confidence, reduce anxiety,* and *increase our sense of control.* Together, these three pieces create a psychological performance preparation trifecta that facilitates our ability to use our skills at the highest level.

Building Confidence

Before we even step into the arena, our mind begins to explore what we expect to go right and what we expect to go wrong. In fact, our brain spends a disproportionate amount of time and energy assessing the potential pitfalls, as those are the areas that could most disrupt our success. For example, you're more likely to spend time and energy thinking about the parts of a presentation your boss won't like than thinking about all the ways it can go well. Your brain, in an effort to prepare you, will distract you from thinking about success. These pitfalls, while real, compound our challenges: they increase anxiety and consequently decrease focus and confidence. An inability to shut down these challenges poses a real difficulty in reaching for an optimal state of automatic, effortless execution. It's a natural human reaction and affects everyone from amateur to elite performers, and if not tamed can easily disrupt our flow and execution.

From a psychological perspective, automaticity is really about having a clear, accurate working mental model of the performance (including our internal experience during the performance). This model is built through applying the type of practice we just covered and hands-on experience, like when you're raising kids or practicing medicine. The more you practice, the stronger or more highly developed your model will become. The better attuned your working model is to the conditions you expect in performance, the better your brain can predict the behaviors that will be most effective during that performance, and thus the better your execution. As we've already explored, some internal stimuli can interfere with this efficient execution, however, so we'll turn our attention to how psychological preparation can mitigate those risks.

We'll begin with what society has held up as the Holy Grail as to how we should feel in pressure-packed situations—*confident*. Unfortunately, this framing of confidence as the way we *should* feel under pressure makes this state even more elusive. We start to think that confidence is just a trait we have or don't have, kind of like talent. But confidence is not a trait; it is a matter of belief. It is a belief in what we are capable of doing, and thus is fluid and can be diminished or added to.

Psychologists call this belief *self-efficacy*. Self-efficacy boils down to the belief that you have the skills necessary to meet the challenge at hand. It comes from five sources:[7]

- mastery experiences;
- past success;
- observing a peer execute well;
- verbal persuasion; and
- using our physiology to reduce anxiety.

Mastery Experiences
Mastery experiences build confidence by helping us notice and process when we're improving. We all experience mastery as we get better at something, but often people tend to minimize or overlook the quality of those experiences or fail to see they are transferable. It's hard to say why we do not appreciate the process of mastery for what it is, as it limits our ability to access mastery as a source of confidence.

Past Success

Past success is simply being able to tap into the past performances when we delivered our best. Reliving those experiences and understanding how we were able to perform gives us the belief that we can deliver again in similar circumstances. When we've been successful before, it's easier to see how we might do it again.

Observing a Peer Execute Well

Many of us have seen a colleague or classmate perform well and thought, "If they can do it, why can't I?" That is a small nudge toward having a more confident performance. Seeing someone else deliver in similar circumstances allows us to identify what worked and what we could do differently, and to learn from them so that when we get on stage, we believe we can do the same. This happens regularly for children, who first watch their friends take a risk on a trampoline and then work up the courage to try it themselves. After seeing a friend who's like them do it, your child is more confident they can do it themselves.

Verbal Persuasion

Verbal persuasion is what's more commonly referred to as "self-talk." Whether you know it or not, you're constantly talking to yourself. Sometimes, this self-talk is about mundane things, like what you are having for dinner. Other times, it's about mistakes or successes. And how you use this self-talk can have a big impact on the way you think, feel, and perform.

Ethan Kross, a leading expert on the science of self-talk, covers a range of techniques performers can use to make their inner voice work for them in his book *Chatter*.[8] When it comes to confidence, there are two techniques to try. The first is to remind yourself of your preparation and how it was designed to help you succeed. The second is to remind yourself of your strengths and positive qualities you can deploy to make your performance a success.

Reducing Anxiety

One element of self-efficacy, or managing our physiology, has a great deal to do with reducing anxiety in psychological preparation. It's hard to feel confident and anxious at the same time. The two states are inversely related: as one goes down, the other goes up. So our physiology can help us or hurt us. If we've trained ourselves to feel ready, poised, and prepared, our physiology can be a great source of confidence. If we feel we have not prepared ourselves at the level we should have, our anxiety and nerves, compounded by negative self-talk, will hurt us.

Psychological preparation helps to reduce this anxiety, which in turn bolsters our confidence. Performance psychologists have worked for a long time on this aspect of preparation, which nearly everyone has experienced—what's been termed "performance anxiety." Performance anxiety is problematic because it redirects our attention and energy away from the task at hand, and typically toward elements of performance we can't control and which may have minimal influence over the total outcome. Our physiology and experience of anxiety are intimately linked. A racing heartbeat, sweaty palms or forehead, and shallow breathing can all be classed as anxiety, which in turn can negatively impact our performance. These same symptoms can also be classed as excitement, care, or determination, which can boost our performance.

Effectively managing our physiology boils down to being able to either find our Individual Zone of Optimal Functioning (IZOF)[9] or frame our physiology more effectively. Your IZOF is your particular place on the Yerkes–Dodson curve (see Figure 6-1) where you perform your best. For some athletes, they want to be calm, cool, and collected heading into competition. For others, they want to be high octane, high energy. But in either case, if your physiology doesn't match what you want to feel, you'll experience a bit of performance anxiety.

Figure 6-1: Yerkes–Dodson Law[10]

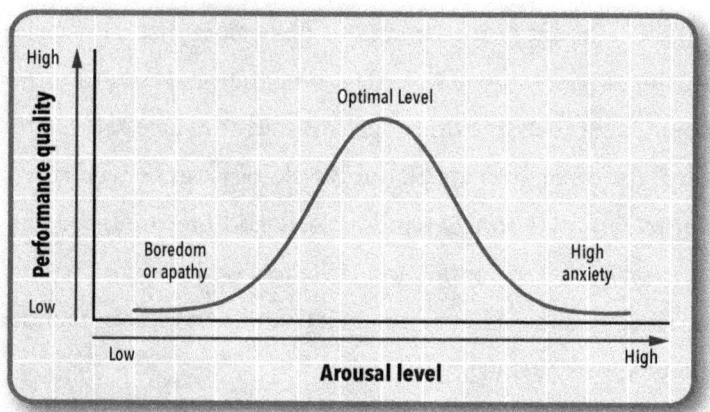

In a moment, you'll be introduced to some techniques you can use to find your IZOF, including increasing your sense of control, using pre-performance routines, and breath work techniques. But in the event that those techniques don't have the maximum impact you'd like, there's one more step you can take. You can change the way you think about what you're feeling.

Reappraisal, or what's sometimes called reframing, is the act of *recategorizing* your current experience into something more adaptive.[11] The physiological markers of anxiety—those sweaty palms and racing heart I mentioned earlier—are also emblematic of excitement. You can choose the category. And by choosing correctly, you can help or hinder your performance.

When I work with professional athletes, one of the first things I teach them is how to appraise their physiology more effectively. We're living in an era where it's common to call any elevated physiology "anxiety." And while labels can help us understand our experience, they can also lead to problems. Instead of seeing it as anxiety, there are four helpful framings I teach my high performers.

The first is seeing the arousal as a sign you care. Nobody gets physiologically activated for something that isn't important to them. Changing from nervousness to care is a powerful switch that gives you a new frame through which to view performance.

The second is seeing the arousal as excitement. You just learned that excitement has the same signature as nervousness. By calling it excitement, you turn a negative into a positive.

You can also note your arousal as a sign of determination. Similar to caring, determination only shows up when we're ready to make something happen. Think of this arousal as a sign that your brain and body are getting you ready to do something effortful (that's what a "stress response" is, after all).

Finally, you can choose to see this arousal as enhancing. Your body is *giving* you what you need to perform—energy! Energy is good. Energy is to be guided and used. And if you do that well, your performance will soar. When you feel all that energy, though, there's one small downside. You need somewhere to direct it, otherwise it can run haywire. For that, we turn to our last step—increasing control—to give our minds a target to focus on and deploy that energy effectively.

Increasing Control

Control is critical for proper psychological preparation. Beyond identifying the "controllables," or the parts of performance we can directly influence, we can influence our overall sense of control by predicting other aspects of performance. This element of psychological preparation is like developing your own performance game plan.

In fact, many performance psychologists develop competition plans with their athletes so that the approach to the game is fully mapped out and easy to follow. Having a clear goal, a defined role, and the ability to anticipate challenges in the future can allow a performer to better tune into the elements of performance that will make the biggest difference. By enabling athletes to focus on the parts of a performance they can control, psychologists help them maximize their sense of what's possible to achieve.

The way we do this part of psychological preparation is by identifying what specifically is required of you in a performance. What type of performance are you delivering? For example, in the case of a public speaker, are you informing, entertaining, or both? What do each of those types of performances demand of a speaker? Understanding the answers to these questions can help you most appropriately gear your practice and psychological preparation to optimal performance. Each public speech or sales pitch won't require the same combination of flair, education, rhythm, fluidity, and knowledge—and that's okay. To truly help yourself optimize, ask yourself what the performance will demand of you and how you can best prepare to deliver that.

You then take that one step further, which is to explore what parts of the performance you can control. For example, a public speaker can't control whether audience members are on their phones, but instead of becoming rattled or distracted by that, the speaker can direct their attention to those who are paying close attention. By focusing on their clear goal (to educate the audience), their defined role (to lead the group in an engaging fashion), and by anticipating potential challenges, the speaker will give themselves the best chance of performing at their best. They've proactively defined what's expected and how to do it and identified obstacles and how to mitigate them. The result is a greater sense of control.

In my work with surgeons, the importance of control comes up a lot. A poor outcome of an intervention is unacceptable. "No issue detected" is the goal for any operation—we want things to go according to plan. So when the results of a procedure are less than optimum, it often creates tension and pressure based on the perception that the surgeon lacked a degree of control.

Surgeries are complicated because the human body is complex. In my coaching after a suboptimal outcome, it's common for the surgeon to focus on what went wrong and for attention to be drawn to "if onlies"—the aspects of the surgery that would've changed the outcome had they gone just a little bit differently. This natural human tendency to reflect on the "if onlies" can lead to self-doubt, though, if they go unchecked.

The if-onlies come up because the surgeons are looking for reasons to understand an undesirable outcome. Whenever that's the case, it's natural to examine things beyond your control, like the condition of the patient when they came in, because it provides an explanation that protects their ego. This is understandable, but not all that useful.

Instead, the surgeon should focus on the things that were within their control. Were they as mentally prepared and focused? Did they check every aspect of the patient's history and data, leaving nothing out? Did they guide their team effectively? Did they have the right instruments ready to go?

Being aware of gaps of things in their control is a learning experience that will influence the surgeon's approach going forward. And, noticing what they did correctly is instructive because it helps them understand what to focus on in the future to maintain a level of high performance in the operating room. When we can attend to what's controllable, we build a repeatable foundation for success.

Preparation in Action

Now that we've explored what goes into purposeful practice and what the science tells us about psychological preparation for optimal performance, it's time to drill into how we make this work for ourselves. Here we'll find a few practical tips I've used with performers to help them adequately prepare for the world's biggest stages.

Pre-Performance Routines

A pre-performance routine is a structured sequence of steps a performer engages in before the big moment to help themselves find their performance sweet spot. Each performer has a physiological state that allows them to function at their best. For some, it may be a calm and deliberate state, while for others it may be an explosive and amped state. There's not a right answer in the absolute sense, but only in the relative sense. It's about what works for *you*. So let's begin with the end in mind.

First, identify what you believe to be your optimal performance state for a given performance. Just pick one to focus on for now. See if you can distill that state into a few active words, such as "calm" or "explosive" or "locked in." Now, make a short list of activities that help you get into that frame of mind. It can be things like listening to music, deep breathing, physical movement, motivational self-talk, or something else.

Now, imagine you're hiking up a hill. By the time you get to the final push to the top, you want to be in your optimal frame of mind. With the list you just made, imagine using those activities as you progressively climb the mountain. Which activity would go best at the base, when you're just getting ready for performance? What about as you get progressively closer to the top? Again, there are no right or wrong answers here—it's just about getting yourself in the optimal position to summit.

Now, give that a try before your next performance: walk yourself through this sequence of steps that facilitate your optimal performance state. Make note of how you feel at each step of the way and whether you're getting closer to or further away from your optimal state. You can always refine the sequence: this is about testing your own hypotheses and helping yourself find your sweet spot.

Mental Contrasting and Implementation Intentions

All performances are going to have obstacles. Rather than simply praying for smooth sailing, psychologists developed a performance tool called *mental contrasting and implementation intentions* that allows us to adequately account for adversity.[12]

Think about an event or goal that is on the horizon. Put yourself in the frame of a performer. To get started using the mental contrasting and implementation intentions tool, make a list of challenges you think you might face in performance. For example, if you're giving a big speech, you might write down things such as the presentation doesn't display, the microphone cuts off, or the crowd doesn't engage. Next, write down what you will do to overcome that hurdle if it happens. So, if your laptop won't link to the room's audio/video technology, what can you do to make sure your presentation performance still goes according to plan? You might have an outline as Plan B, so that you are prepared for any eventuality. Finally, close out by making these intentions into if–then statements, such as: "If the presentation doesn't display, then I'll use my written outline to guide me through my speech."

Do this for the hurdles you can anticipate and you'll be ready when adversity strikes.

Process Goals

As a part of purposeful practice, it can be helpful to set goals that define a narrow focus and intention for our efforts. Psychologists call the goals in these situations *process goals*. A process goal is a small step you can take that demonstrates real progress on your path to mastery and performance preparation.

To illustrate, imagine you are giving a big sales pitch. A process goal might be to work on making better eye contact as you pitch, so that you're more connected to the customer. Process goals help orient us toward what we can control and give us a clear target to focus on.

Process goals can be particularly helpful in the preparation stage. A process goal is simply a goal focused on the improvement of a specific technique or tactic. By setting process goals, you're leveraging one of the most powerful tools athletes use to improve their performance. Research suggests that the act of setting a process goal significantly boosts performance.[13]

Breathing

A simple tool you can use to help yourself find your optimal performance state is breathing. The breath is a shortcut to our physiology; it can be used to calm us down or ramp us up. In the case of performance, however, it's rare that we need to be amped up further, so we'll focus here on how to relax and allow the performance to come to us.

To calm ourselves down, slow and controlled breathing is one of the best tricks we have. Two examples of controlled breathing are box breathing and 4-7-8 breathing.

Box breathing involves breathing in through your nose for a count of four, holding your breath for a count of four, breathing out of your mouth for a count of four, and holding the out-breath at the bottom for a count of four. Simple repetition of this exercise gives us increased control over our breathing and can help slow down our heart rate and calm our racing thoughts.

Another tool that can be used to relax is 4-7-8 breathing. Similar to box breathing, 4-7-8 breathing is about a controlled pattern of breathing: count to four as you breathe in, hold for a count of seven, and breathe out for a count of eight.

Both of these exercises can be used to quickly change our physiology and find our optimal state. In general, longer exhales than inhales will help you calm down, and shorter exhales than inhales will help you ramp up.

Identifying Controllables

A final technique we'll discuss to help yourself be ready is to identify the aspects of your performance that you can control and the aspects of your performance you can't control. Once you've identified what you can't control, resolve to let those things go. With the list of what we can control in performance, we can use our purposeful practice to make sure we are ready to deliver across the full range of controllables.

For example, in delivering a big sales pitch, some things the salesperson can control that influence the performance are the speed of the delivery, degree of eye contact, clarity of communication, and quality of information in the slide deck. (Each of these could be turned into process goals too.) Practicing the presentation would include experimenting with voice inflections, amount of information to be shared, questions to be asked of the audience, and assessing the overall pitch to determine which elements best meet the desired outcomes of the performance.

Outside of the salesperson's control are things like how attentive the audience is, the misfunctioning of technology, and poor weather which prevents some people from attending. By choosing to not let those pieces of the equation influence a performance by distracting focus, you increase your odds of success.

* * *

Readiness is a combination of purposeful practice, deliberate practice, and psychological preparation. With the skills we just reviewed and varied, purposeful rehearsal of the skills we need to execute, we can position ourselves to be ready to deliver our best when it matters most. Good readiness training is fairly simple, but it's not easy. It requires discipline and commitment to vary our practice conditions, to keep putting in time when we may or may not see improvement, and to actively work on our mindset that facilitates peak performance.

Although not explicitly linked to the three clear goals of psychological preparation I've just outlined, there is one more critical factor that can help us perform our best under pressure: *framing the performance*. Appropriately framing the performance and putting it into context can be the difference between optimal and suboptimal performance. Let me explain.

When taking a test in school, you've experienced the framing problem first-hand. How many all-nighters or cramming sessions have you pulled to prepare for a test, because achieving an "A" was critical for maintaining your GPA or getting into a college of your choice? Perhaps getting an "A" was simply a matter of living up to your own expectations. At the time, nothing seems as important as the test and the result. And yet, I've never met a single person who has been asked about a test grade they received. I've been guilty of this myself. I thought that the tests I took in school would define my future. Yet, as I write this, not a single person has ever asked me about a test grade, my GPA, or anything else related to my academic performance.

This illustrates a common performance problem during preparation: we mis-frame the performance, making it loom larger in our minds than necessary. This isn't to say that we should minimize the value of preparation, performing well, and progressing. On the contrary, realistically framing our performance as a current measure of our skill, a place where we get to test if our practice is paying off and not as some absolute measure of our ability (or worse yet, quality as a human being) can be the difference between tipping into performance anxiety and finding our sweet spot. It's important to find the right framing for our performance. Explain why the performance matters, what it's really a measure of, and see if you can identify any negative consequences if you don't quite deliver. Chances are those negative consequences, if any, will be short-lived and quickly forgotten.

Purposeful practice allows you to experiment with how you perform under varying conditions and to ready yourself for the dynamic conditions of any performance. Psychological preparation can help you create three critical states for performance: increased feelings of confidence, increased sense of control, and a reduced state of anxiety. The best performers under pressure know that to get the most out of themselves during a performance, they have to prepare for possible futures and how they will respond to potential adversities, and actively cultivate the thoughts and feelings they want to have as they enter the arena. They need to be ready. Whether your arena is a board room or a football field, performing your best when the lights come on starts well before the games begin, with preparedness.

PREPARING FOR RACE DAY

Imagine a Formula 1 driver preparing to race a new course, like the one that just opened in Las Vegas near The Strip. The driver's first step would be to get physically ready to perform.

That would mean that they'd engage in practice that involved repetition, variation, and representativeness. They'd practice with repetition by doing laps on their home training ground. The driver could introduce variation by practicing under different weather conditions or by adjusting the time of their training. They could close their training regimen with representativeness by taking a few laps around the course in Las Vegas and reviewing the course via film.

As our driver starts to get ready psychologically, they turn their attention to increasing confidence, narrowing their focus on the controllables, and reducing performance anxiety. They review their past successes and wins, make note of the progress they've made in training, and speak optimistically to themselves about what's possible. They view their nerves as excitement.

The racer then builds a competition plan, identifying their goals, race-day targets, and how they want to drive on race day. They focus on what they can control—the speed with which they take corners, how aggressive they are—and let go of the rest, like whether or not a pit crew member will repeat a past mistake. After all, they've made a plan for what to do if the pit crew messes up, using mental contrasting and implementation intentions.

Finally, on the day of the race, they go through their pre-performance routine to put themselves in their IZOF. As the race begins, they're in the best condition they can be in to perform. The odds are in their favor.

* * *

In the next chapter, we'll discuss Principle #2: Immersion. I frame immersion in an equation: **awareness + focus + commitment = immersion**. To be at your best, you need to be fully locked in. Let's look at how.

ENDNOTES

1. Damien Farrow and Samuel J. Robertson, "Development of a Skill Acquisition Periodisation Framework for High-Performance Sport." *Sports Medicine* 47 (2017): 1043-1054.

2. K. Anders Ericsson, Ralf T. Krampe, and Clemens Tesch-Römer, "The Role of Deliberate Practice in the Acquisition of Expert Performance." *Psychological Review* 100(3) (1993/7).

3. Jamie C. Brehaut et al., "Practice Feedback Interventions: 15 Suggestions for Optimizing Effectiveness." *Annals of Internal Medicine* 164 (2016): 435-441. https://doi.org/10.7326/M15-2248.

4. Elizabeth L. Bjork and Robert A. Bjork, "Making Things Hard on Yourself, but in a Good Way: Creating Desirable Difficulties to Enhance Learning." In M. A. Gernsbacher, R. W. Pew, L. M. Hough, and J. R. Pomerantz (Eds.), *Psychology and the Real World: Essays Illustrating Fundamental Contributions to Society* (London: Worth Publishers/Macmillan Learning, 2011): 55-64.

5. Wayne D. Gray and John K. Lindstedt, "Plateaus, Dips, and Leaps: Where to Look For Inventions and Discoveries during Skilled Performance." *Cognitive Science* 41(7) (2017): 1838-1870.

6. Rob Gray, R. "Movement Automaticity in Sport." In J. Baker & D. Farrow (Eds.), *Routledge Handbook of Sport Expertise* (London: Routledge/Taylor & Francis, 2015): 74-83.

7. Albert Bandura, "Self-Efficacy Mechanism in Human Agency." *American Psychologist* 37(2) (1982): 122-147. https://doi.org/10.1037/0003-066X.37.2.122

8. Ethan Kross, *The Voice in Our Head, Why It Matters, and How to Harness It* (New York: Crown, 2022).

9. Yuri L. Hanin, "Emotions and Athletic Performance: Individual Zones of Optimal Functioning Model." In D. Smith & M. Bar-Eli (Eds.), *Essential Readings in Sport and Exercise Psychology* (London: Human Kinetics, 2007): 55-73.

10. Ibid.

11. S.W. Gangestad and M. Snyder, "Self-Monitoring: Appraisal and Reappraisal." *Psychological Bulletin* 126(4) (2000): 530.

12. Gabriele Oettingen and Peter M. Gollwitzer, "Strategies of Setting and Implementing Goals: Mental Contrasting and Implementation Intentions." In J. E. Maddux and J. P. Tangney (Eds.), *Social Psychological Foundations of Clinical Psychology* (London: The Guildford Press, 2010): 114-135.

13. Ollie Williamson et al., "The Performance and Psychological Effects of Goal Setting in Sport: A Systematic Review and Meta-Analysis." *International Review of Sport and Exercise Psychology* (2022): 1-29.

PRINCIPLE #2:

Immersion

You have to be able to center yourself, to let all of your emotions go. Don't forget that you play with your soul as well as your body.

– Kareem Abdul-Jabbar

If you've prepared well, you're now ready to enter the arena. The next step toward any great performance is to be fully present, **immersed** in the experience of the game. You have to *lean in, commit,* and *give yourself over* to the game.

The only moment that performers can control is here and now. Thoughts of the past or future, what just happened or what might happen next, what we just screwed up and how we can make it right in a few moments—all of these distract from what ultimately enables the best to deliver under pressure: a full, complete immersion in the moment.

You can think of immersion as a simple formula: **awareness + focus + commitment = immersion**. And the skill of immersion can be coached and trained.

Immersion is firstly about awareness, which involves recognizing our feelings and thoughts and how they connect to our behavior. Awareness is like the starting point on your GPS; the other elements of immersion, focus and commitment, are like selecting a route and staying the course. You need to begin with a sense of where your mind is starting, so you know where to take it.

Taking it to the right place is about the self-regulation of attention. It's how we maintain our focus on the task at hand and how easily we make the necessary shifts between a focus on ourselves, others, and the environment as performance unfolds. Each of these data sources—ourselves, others, and the environment—has rich information about how we're performing and what we should do next.

Commitment requires giving a full effort and not quitting until the performance is over. Commitment means leaning in and taking risks, knowing that your effort may not work out the way you want. It's a recognition that the most important thing you can do for any great performance is to leave it all out on the field, in the boardroom, or in the concert hall. I'd like to quote the great Walter Payton here:

> Another thing Coach [Bob Hill at Jackson State] was big on was not running out-of-bounds unless you were hit out. That had always been my style. I'd say, I'm not gonna run out-of-bounds before I hit somebody first. I wanted to make them feel me a little. I took great pride in that. A lot of guys are afraid of injury. Personally, I like contact. I enjoyed it. My whole thing was, I'll give it to them before they give it to me. It's a system that works. Every play, I wanted to go full blast, 110, 120 percent.
>
> One of Coach Hill's mottos, one I took to heart, was "Never die easy." I took that as a motto for my game and my life. ... Make that linebacker pay. Make him earn your death. ... It's okay to lose, to die, but don't die without trying, without giving it your best.[1]

In the previous chapter, we focused on preparation and practice. Immersion is the natural next step once the preparation is over for the time being. It's about getting into the flow of the performance as quickly as possible. No matter how impeccable our preparation is, it's unlikely that we accounted for the many permutations performance can throw at us. Immersion is what allows us to respond to the unique demands of this performance, by directing our focus where we need it to be and staying in the here and now as performance unfolds. *Taking any performance moment-by-moment is perhaps the most important step we can take to being our best when it matters most.*

We'll need other skills along the way to help us perform our best, but if we aren't aware of where we are starting (what we're thinking and feeling), what route to take (where and when to place our attention), and where we want to go (staying committed to the goals of performance), the rest of the skills won't matter, because we'll be going nowhere fast.

* * *

WHAT LEGENDARY IMMERSION LOOKS LIKE

Down 28–3 to the Atlanta Falcons in the 51st Super Bowl, Tom Brady, (arguably) the greatest quarterback of all time, wasn't thinking about putting enough points on the board to win the game. When you're down by twenty-five points at the end of the third quarter in the big game, it's almost a foregone conclusion that the game is over. That the trophy is going home with the other guys. In these instances, it's a natural human experience to think about the end—the end of the pain, the end of the season, the end of the opportunity, the end of the game. Our minds rush us through to get it over with. Losing hurts, and nobody wants to stay in that space psychologically. We are taken out of the moment and into a magical future where the embarrassment is over.

As everyone watching started to wonder how even one of the greatest to ever do it might come back from a whooping like this, Tom Brady was focused on one thing: "get one score."

The magic of a focus on just one score illustrates the magic of immersion. Rather than worrying about how it might turn out, the lost opportunity, or starting over, attention shifts to the here and now. To the very thing, and only thing, one of the best quarterbacks of all time could do to stave off embarrassment. The only thing that might give his team a chance to win.

Tom's message was that the only way out was to go in.

In recounting the game, Brady said that his focus for the team was to "maintain our poise, maintain our execution, do our jobs"; in other words, to immerse fully in the performance. To be aware of the situation, but not let it define you. To shift attention to the moment and commit to executing as best as they could.

Slowly but surely, that immersion brought Brady and the New England Patriots back into the game. A mere fifteen minutes later, the deficit had been erased and the game was headed to overtime. By that point, the Patriots were so engrossed in the game that they seemed unstoppable.

Sure enough, the Patriots received the ball first in overtime and marched seventy-five yards in just under four minutes to write a new chapter in football history. Brady too made history as the winningest QB of all time.

THE SCIENCE BEHIND IMMERSION

Brady's ability to immerse himself in the game and deliver at a high level is built on diligent preparation and facilitated by three processes we're about to explore: *awareness, attentional focus,* and *commitment.*

Awareness

Becoming fully immersed in the performance starts with your awareness. To perform well consistently, you need to have an awareness of your goals and actions; your thinking, feeling, and physiology; and the demands of your performance environment. The better the understanding you have of each of these dimensions of your world, the easier it will be for you to adjust your behavior, and performance, accordingly.

Awareness is the starting point for the journey to peak performance. Awareness asks us, "What are my goals right now?" and "How am I feeling?" or "Where is my attention?" The answers to these questions give us a sense of where we're beginning, which is the first step to knowing where you want to go.

Awareness is also about understanding the context of the performance as fully as possible. It's about being aware of moment-to-moment changes in your physiology, changes in the game, or changes in the physiology of teammates and opponents. If you're not aware of the situation you're in, it's hard to lead others, make clear decisions, and execute the game plan.

Awareness is built by learning to guide our attention to the different features of our experience. Whatever we attend to is what we're aware of at that time, and that awareness and attention guides our actions. To build our awareness, we have to learn to guide our attention in a manner that serves us. This requires a method that allows us to scan for and find meaningful information from our body (mental and physical) and in the external environment. We can then determine what information will contribute to a better performance in the moment. Information that is not useful is discarded.

Imagine, for a moment, a dark stage before a show. Then, a spotlight comes on and starts moving around the stage. As it moves, it highlights different elements of the set—perhaps a tree in the background, the night sky, or a building—guiding your attention to what's important for you to understand the performance as a whole. Awareness and attention function much like that spotlight, highlighting relevant information and allowing you to piece together a gestalt of the environment so that you have a mastery of the context in which the performance takes place.

Focus

Our brain is constantly maintaining a working model of ourselves and the world around us by actively trying to predict what is happening.[2,3] That's the fundamental value of awareness—it keeps us fully apprised of the situation. This internal working model allows us to maintain a sense of who we are, how we are feeling, and what's required of us, as well as a sense of constancy in the world. When there is a mismatch between what we expect and what actually happens, our brain detects this gap and uses that information to adjust our model. That's the crux of expert performance—quickly and accurately updating our models so we can stay most closely aligned with the demands of the task at hand.

The information we detect varies based on where we place our attention. In fact, some research suggests that detecting this variation is attention.[4] You can move your attention around: internally and externally, broad or narrow. Once you've determined where to put your attention, you need to then take that awareness a step further and turn it into focus.

A classic example of how attention can be impacted by what we choose to focus on is humorously and effectively illustrated in an experiment conducted by Daniel J. Simons, who calls it The Monkey Business Illusion. You can find the video on YouTube.

When you begin watching the group of people passing a basketball back and forth, you are asked to count how many times players in white shirts exchange passes. This simple instruction guides your attention and determines what to look for in the performance. It gives you a goal to focus on and permission to narrow your attention. Your brain now knows that what matters most is the number of basketball passes the players in white shirts make. You don't need to have your attention diverted by the players who are wearing black shirts, for example. It's simple: just stay focused on the players wearing white and count the number of passes they make.

You, like most people who have watched the video, were likely able to accurately record the number of passes thrown by the white team. And you, like most people who have watched the video, likely missed something extraordinary. About halfway through the video, a person in a gorilla costume walks into the midst of the players, pounds their chest, and walks off the opposite side of the playing area. A couple of other things happened: one of the players on the black team leaves the playing area and a curtain that serves as a backdrop changes color. But you, just like those who participated in Dr. Simons' experiment, were not set up to be attuned to or aware of anything like the appearance of a gorilla. Your focus was somewhere else—on your goal. When we focus like this, it's both a blessing and a curse. We can ignore irrelevant information with incredible accuracy, but we can also miss disruptive changes in the scenery that might be worth catching.

Fortunately, in the case of the gorilla, we don't miss anything important. But if you're anything like me, you've had the experience of being so focused on something that you lost track of time, missed a meal or an important call, or just flat-out forgot something. That's the power of focus applied to a goal.

In fact, that's the precursor to immersion. You're so involved in the task at hand that you miss other (and not-so-important) information.

Internal Focus and External Focus

To maximize our performance, then, we must get ahold of our attention. We have to learn to guide it to our most important goals and keep it there. In a bit, I'll introduce you to a set of science-backed tools you can use to catch the gorilla when you need to and let it go or ignore it when you don't. But before we turn our attention (no pun intended) to the tools and tactics, we need to dial in on how to focus.

As a spotlight is to awareness, a magnifying glass is to focus. Once we've directed our attention where we need it to be, focus allows us to dial up or down the intensity of that attention. The second step of the immersion equation—focus—allows us to further attune to the unique demands of the performance and make sure we're detecting the signals we need to adapt as the performance unfolds.

Research confirms that as we narrow our attention, the speed of our processing increases.[5] Once we're aware of where we'd like to head, dialing in allows us to get there more efficiently—faster and with fewer errors. But that's not all. As the efficiency of processing increases, our execution becomes more automatic. We start to feel our preparation kicking in, and we increase our sense of immersion in the activity. We start to lose track of time and lose ourselves in the activity.

If we want to supercharge our immersion, where we place our attention matters. There are two considerations here: internal stimuli and external stimuli.

What do we mean by internal stimuli? We could pay attention to the rapidity of our heartbeat or breathing and use this information to adjust to what the performance demands of us. Think of a golfer about to make a game-winning putt. Anxiety is not a friend. Though we wouldn't want to direct attention to those internal stimuli, if they happened to grab our attention, we'd want a tool we could use, like breathwork, to slow that arousal down and increase focus in the right place—on what's in front of them.

The ideal place for the golfer to focus is on the external, like the lie of the green. Perhaps it is damp, and the golfer has to assess the effect of dampness on the ball's speed, or there's a slight incline to account for. What the research tells us is that to optimize our performance, the best thing we can do is maintain our attention externally.[6] Though we might shift our attention internally at times during performance, maintaining our focus on the target—whether that's engaging an audience, shooting a basket, or caring for a newborn—allows us to execute most efficiently.

Coach's Corner: Tips on Leveraging External Focus

Placing our focus externally essentially helps us get our mind out of our own way. This external attention means our mind spends less time processing internal stimuli or experiences that can get in the way of our performance, like a recent mistake or the thoughts in our head. Here are some tips to keep your focus on the task at hand and the environment you're in. Doing so allows us to respond more flexibly in the moment (more on that in the next chapter) and increases our likelihood of successful adaptation. It also turns out that this external attention increases the skill with which we perform:[7]

- Ask yourself, "What's important now?" (WIN)

- Use a focal cue, like one feature of your environment that you can come back to (e.g., a screen showing your slides in the presentation or an opponent lining up across the line of scrimmage in a game).

- Focus on someone or something outside of you and notice its features, such as color, shape, and texture.

To recap, we've learned that a relatively narrow, external focus increases the efficiency and fluidity with which we respectively process information and then execute. These two elements combined can lead us to feel as though our performance is more automatic and effortless which, although not an explicit goal of training, is an implicit goal of practice. We want to develop our skills so much during the readiness phase that, by the time we walk on stage, the performance flows from us executing what we've trained to do, rather than having our minds intervene in the moment. This is why to be at our best requires spending hours rehearsing the same movements and activities, so that by the time the bright lights come on, our body almost instinctually knows how to execute and we can use the extra cognitive resources to process tactics and strategies during a performance.

Perhaps nowhere is this focus more evident than the penalty kick in soccer. If you've watched any of the last World Cups—men's or women's—you've noticed the intensity of the penalty. It's one ball, one attacker, one goalie, and one shot. The best penalty-takers shift their focus quickly between two areas: where they want to kick the ball, and where the goalie is located. If you watch an all-time great like Leo Messi, you'll notice that he uses his run up to the ball, paired with an external focus on the goalie, to manipulate the situation in his favor.

In these instances, the striker is at a huge advantage. The goalie is essentially forced to guess, given the strength and speed of the kicks of a modern striker. But the shooter can try to get the goalie to guess early, and by monitoring the right external cues make their performance much easier.

For instance, in a late-game penalty when he was playing for FC Barcelona, Messi was called on to take a shot. After he places the ball, the camera pans to his face. You see him take one deep, centering breath. He opens his eyes and begins his jog toward the ball.

As he's jogging, he notices the goalie bend and lean to one side. This action—an external cue—tells Messi exactly where to shoot. He slows down his movement for a split second, lets the goalie commit, and calmly kicks the ball along the ground into the open corner, just like making a pass at practice.

Commitment

In sport, you'll hear coaches use phrases like "trust your training." This "trust" factor might best be understood as commitment, or the process of fully giving oneself over to the performance and relying on the preparation beforehand to facilitate optimal execution. Let's unpack that for a moment.

Research shows that commitment shows up in several ways in sport: through perseverance, motivation, self-determination, a desire to prove oneself, pursuing excellence, doing one's best, and working on weaknesses.[8] Underneath all of these themes is one simple idea: the performer who fully commits to giving their full effort is likely to achieve more and feel better about their performance if they fall short. They're also more likely to be motivated, persevere in the face of difficulty, and pursue excellence.

This idea of psychological commitment is important for several reasons. First, the reality for most athletes—even those at the top of their game—is that they rarely step onto the field or court at 100 percent. This is likely true for you too. More realistically, the best performers aim on any given day to give the maximum of what they have on that day. It might only be 80 percent of their maximum capacity, but their commitment allows them to give 100 percent of that 80 percent, instead of worrying about what it means to not be able to give the missing 20 percent. You'd be surprised at the number of performers across industries that spend so much time and energy on the 20 percent that's missing that they fail to give what they have.

Second, performances rarely go exactly according to plan. By giving a full effort and committing to doing their best, performers are able to use their energy to efficiently respond to setbacks, novelty, or adversity, instead of wasting their mental energy waffling back and forth in their mind about every bump in the road. The committed performer responds by doubling down and enhancing effort, rather than wondering how things are going in the moment or splitting their attention between the present and the past or future. The uncommitted performer sees mistakes as a sign of an inadequate ability and questions whether or not they should continue.[9]

Finally, this increase in commitment and giving our full effort improves our odds of entering what psychologists call "flow" or "clutch" states. For us to enter these states of total absorption in the task at hand, we need to be fully present and all in. While psychological commitment can't guarantee that we enter these peak performance states, the absence of psychological commitment all but guarantees that we won't be entering them as we perform. Research suggests that for the high-skilled worker to get into flow in any setting off the field, it takes *grit*, or the willingness to persist even in the face of adversity.[10] In this research, grit and commitment fill the role of giving the worker extra motivation when encountering obstacles, essentially allowing them to continue drilling down in their focus until the flow state emerges.

IMMERSION IN ACTION

Though we won't have performances like Tom Brady each time we fully immerse ourselves, immersion gives us the best chance to perform at a high level. It's hard to do well when we are only halfway committed, with divided attention and focus between performance and what we have going on at home or what we ate for lunch earlier, or when we're not aware of what the situation demands of us. It can be difficult to separate what's going on in our personal life from the demands of a performance, yet doing so is necessary to get the most out of yourself when you need to. To perform your best, most of the time, you have to jump in with both feet.

Building Awareness: Mindfulness Meditation

Self-awareness is what allows you to recognize if you've fully jumped in or if you're holding back. That's one of the areas where you can benefit from having a coach, whether you're an athlete or a businessperson. But beyond coaching, there are several other ways you can elevate your self-awareness. With regular practice, you'll find yourself more present and aware. You'll find that self-awareness leads to a cascading down, to focus, commitment, and ultimately, immersion.

An ideal first step for building self-awareness is practicing mindfulness meditation. In a regular mindfulness practice, we pick one object that we place our focus on and, for some time, observe that object in a nonattached, nonjudgmental way. We can do this for a few minutes at a time, or longer. Inevitably, no matter how long we practice our mind will do what it is best at and get distracted. This distraction is actually a good thing—it presents an opportunity for us to recognize what has pulled us out of the moment and has taken over our attention. You can think about this as doing two mental reps, such as strength training. Every time you detach from a distraction and return to the present, that's two reps for strengthening the connection with the here and now.

In her book *Peak Mind,* Dr. Amishi Jha highlights how mindfulness bolsters three critical aspects of our attention: what she calls the "flashlight," (focus), "floodlight," (awareness), and "the juggler."[11] The flashlight is our ability to zoom in and focus on important details—to recognize what's important and emphasize it. The floodlight is our ability to broaden our attention—to zoom back out, search for other relevant information, be aware of our surroundings, and determine our next step. And finally, the juggler is what neuroscientists call our central executive, the part of our brain that holds goal-directed information in mind so we can plan and execute. With regular mindfulness training these elements of attention are strengthened, such that we can keep our goals clearly in focus, find relevant information, and zoom in to act as needed, moving effortlessly between the phases to guide our behavior.

There are apps you can use to practice mindfulness meditation—Insight

Timer, Headspace, Calm, and more all work to teach you the foundations of mindfulness. If you want to up your game, there's technology out there that can give you feedback on your level of presence and help you refocus, often called "biofeedback" or "neurofeedback." I'd recommend saving that for after you've practiced for some time. And, if you're not an app person, that's totally fine. Just sit in a quiet place, close your eyes, and start to notice and pay attention to your breath. Each time you get distracted, just redirect your attention back to your breathing. Start with just a couple of minutes and work your way up over time.

Mindfulness is one of the first techniques I teach nearly every performer with whom I work, from C-suite executives to professional athletes to new parents. In my work with a CEO and new father, for example, we uncovered that he was struggling with persistent thoughts about the development of his child. Of course, being preoccupied with your child's development is normal. It's a sign of love and care. But for this new father, it was actually limiting his ability to be present with his child, and as a result, his sense of connection and identity as the father.

The main culprit here is called cognitive fusion. Sometimes, our thoughts seem so real to us that they metaphorically blind us to anything else, pulling us out of the present moment and into a narrative that we can't seem to shake. We end up *fused* to a story, instead of being present in the moment.

Yet nothing is more important to a new parent than quality time with their child. To be there but not *be there* is painful. We had to find a way to get him present, and mindfulness was our tool of choice. It worked because it trained him to be aware of his thoughts and feelings, be aware when he was present or not, and be aware of when he needed to redirect his attention. Through a simple two-week plan, we were able to center his mind more effectively and train him to let go of the unhelpful narratives in his head and be more present with his son. Mindfulness is powerful because it can make a huge difference in as little as twelve minutes per day.[12]

PRINCIPLE #2: Immersion

As you increase your awareness with mindfulness practice, you'll naturally start to find that you feel a greater sense of control over where you direct your attention. That's one of the added benefits of a sustained mindfulness practice, and you can take mindfulness practice even farther by introducing object-focused meditations. Like a breath meditation, object-focused meditation involves paying attention to a particular thing—in this case, an object of our choosing—for a period of time. As you pay attention, see if you can really tune in to the physical properties of the object, without judgment. For example, you might choose to focus on a garden. Focus on the texture of the blooms, the spectrum of color, and the fragrance of the flowers. Do this without judging the handiwork of the gardener, perhaps where you would have added variety and that sort of thing. Extending our mindfulness practice beyond our body is a great way to practice the skills we need to facilitate deeper attention and focus.

We can extend this approach to performance itself with a technique called "focal cueing." As you now know, placing your attention on what's happening in the environment is the best way to facilitate peak performance—the environment holds the clues to solving the performance puzzle. One way to help anchor our attention to the environment is to prime ourselves with words or cues that direct our attention in that way. For a speaker, for example, a good focal cue might be eye contact with someone in the audience or a point at the back of the room that they can return to as needed. What's important is that these cues are within the performer's control and accessible, and help them to engage in the environment more effectively. In doing so, they prime their minds to focus on what's most important for performance.

As with mindfulness practice, the most important part of engaging in these focal cueing or object meditation exercises is to practice redirecting your attention when you find your mind has wandered. People spend up to 50 percent of their time thinking about the future, so it's only a matter of time before our mind wanders off the turquoise-green glacial lake we've chosen for our object meditation and begins to poke us with the day's to-do list or what we want to have for lunch. Again, the distraction itself is not inherently problematic, because the gains in attention strength come from detaching and returning to the object of focus. Just keep doing your mental reps, and like strength training, you'll find that your level of attention improves over time.

Monitoring

A second step we can take to enhance our self-awareness is a form of journaling called monitoring. Monitoring is about more regularly and systematically making a note of what you are thinking and how you are feeling (emotionally and physiologically) before, during, and after different events in your daily life.

The goal is to start to identify patterns in our thinking and feeling. For example, we might find that a conversation with a boss or a coach tends to provoke anxiety beforehand and a racing, cluttered mind during the conversation. We're relieved when the conversation's over. We can then take these notes a step further and compare and contrast what our responses have been in those critical moments, such as the ways we try to calm our mind during the conversation and how that does or does not help performance. The goal of monitoring is to create a nonjudgmental approach to understanding our own behavior and the psychological factors that lead us closer to, or from, our ideal performance state of immersion.

After two to three weeks of regular monitoring, you'll begin to gain some clarity on the different factors influencing your performance. As you get a better sense of what is facilitating or debilitating in the moment, you can develop strategies to enhance what works and correct what doesn't. For example, if you find that listening to music before a big meeting helps you to feel more energized, you might choose to leave yourself time to listen to your favorite song or two before big events. If you find that having coffee too late in the morning tends to lead to a racing heart and thus makes you feel more anxious and struggle to focus, you might choose to swap that coffee for a herbal tea. The goal is to use this data to refine our approach and get closer to an optimal state for performance.

Going All In

The final piece of the immersion equation is commitment. Most people have had the experience of their heart "not being in it" or their mind "being elsewhere." These two states are what athletes work to overcome—anything less than full presence and commitment is likely to lead to underwhelming performance or worse, such as costing the team the game. Thankfully, we can borrow a couple of tools from the domain of sport to help us better manage this ambivalence and give our best effort.

The first technique we can leverage is to appreciate the sanctity of performance. While this may sound a bit trite, the best performers have a consistent approach and set of steps that they implement before performing, culminating in a state of full presence and commitment to the task at hand. Yes, every game or performance is an opportunity for the performer to demonstrate their skill hone their craft, and showcase their love for what they do. But they know that the performance is not a test of their self-worth. They keep their perspective by not making it any bigger or smaller than it is, but they do treat it like it matters.

There have undoubtedly been times when you have felt you were not at your best during a performance. Sometimes you have to do things you don't want to, such as giving a presentation when you feel sick or tired. However, going all in and being committed will help you make your best effort.

As we discussed in the last chapter, athletes also leverage a combination of goal-setting, mental contrasting, and implementation intentions to raise their levels of commitment. Whether or not you write your goals down or use a goal-setting framework like SMART goals, everyone has something they are trying to achieve in a performance. If your performance is raising a child, your goal is likely to raise the happiest, healthiest child you can. If your performance is a surgical procedure, your goal is a full recovery for your patient. Even if you haven't explicitly named your goal prior to competition, it can be helpful to get really clear on what you're hoping to accomplish in this performance as a starting point. If using a goal-setting framework, like SMART or SMARTER goals, helps you, that's a wonderful step to take, but for the purposes of immersion it's not necessary. For immersion, we just need to have a clear goal we're aiming for as a starting point.

Once the clear goal has been identified, athletes go through a process of identifying obstacles and how they'll overcome them to reach their goal. This is the crux of what coaches do with athletes when game-planning. The goal is to win the game; the game plan is a series of steps athletes can take to overcome the obstacles—for example, the aggressiveness of their opponent and the unique aspects of their strategy. This allows the athletes to go forward with full force, focused on their goals and the strategies they need to use to be successful.

You can use this same process to facilitate your own performance. Before you get into the thick of it, see if you can identify any obstacles you may hit and the steps you can take to overcome them. This process does not need to be drawn out or complicated. Simply identifying the major obstacles you're likely to encounter as you proceed and the strategies you need to keep moving forward will allow you to give your full effort and attention to the performance, without looking over your shoulder to make sure nothing goes wrong.

This strategy was never more important than when I went to work with the Army Rangers at Fort Bragg. The group I met with was engaged in live demolition training. They were taking explosives and simulating entering or destroying a building and securing a target. As you can imagine, under such extreme conditions, you can't be half in. If you're not sure about committing to demolish something, there's no way to execute the mission at the highest level.

As we started talking about the strategies they used to coordinate and perform together, the main theme that emerged was the centrality of the mission. A sole focus on the goal and sticking to the plan allowed them to home in on the clear steps they needed to take to succeed. Each mission had contingency plans or steps the Rangers could take should something go wrong. But at the core of the mission was a simple goal of finishing the job.

When you're assessing your own level of commitment, consider the centrality of the mission. If it's important to you, it's going to require a lot of you. If you're going to give a lot, have a plan for what to do if it doesn't go according to plan. As Mike Tyson said, "Everyone has a plan until they get punched in the face."

* * *

Now you have the techniques you need to bring yourself fully into your performance. Although you may not be 100 percent every time, immersion allows you to maximize what you do have to give. In my years working with high performers, immersion has become one of the most important states to cultivate. I have yet to hear a great performer wish that they gave less effort, were less present and attentive, or less committed to a performance. Elite athletes don't hedge. They give their best and don't shy away from the result, taking to heart whatever lesson there may be to learn before moving forward. If you want to be your best when it matters most, there's only one way forward—going all in.

ARI, THE CHESS CHAMPION

When I was growing up, I was a decent chess player. I went to tournaments and competed. But I was nothing compared to my youngest brother, Ari, who seemed to have a natural knack for the game and a better understanding of the possible permutations of the board. He also had a mindset that allowed him to make the most of each competition, rising through the ranks to be Top 5 in the state before he turned ten.

Here's what made him so successful.

When Ari was in the tournament, he was fully in each game, here and now. He was able to let go of past losses and tough defeats by better opponents. He understood that being his best required him to be with each game.

Chess tournaments are stressful. There's a lot of pressure on the players, not to mention the audience (family members and past champions), live streaming and bright lights. These are all potential distractions that are outside the player's control and which can impact the player's concentration and decision making.

Once you make a move in chess, it's done. You push the clock and you can't go back. You have to wait, even if you realize you've made a mistake, until it's your turn again. You have to quickly process new data, make a decision, and go forward before time runs out.

I think what really made Ari an elite player wasn't his openings, but his ability to respond almost effortlessly to novelty and setbacks, instead of using his mental energy hemming and hawing about a past move he made. He doubled down on effort, kept his focus on the board in front of him, and became one of the best in our state quickly by immersing himself in the game.

* * *

The same thing that helped my youngest brother helped one of the all-time great running backs in the NFL, Walter Payton. Payton had, in his estimation, a horrible rookie season. Here is what he said about his performance:

> I think a lot can be learned from my rookie year. As a team we definitely had some tough years to follow, but none was worse than the first year. We were 4–10 and I gained only 679 yards. It was a bad year for the team and me individually.
>
> But I knew that even though nothing was happening immediately, that if I continued to exert maximum effort, if I continued to work

> hard, if I kept a positive attitude and I continued to work with my teammates, good things could happen. Sometimes you learn more through adversity than success, and my rookie year was proof of that. ...
>
> There is a famous line: "Tough times don't last; tough people do." Well, it's true. It is also true you need to go through some tough times to prove you are a tough person. ... But the faith I kept through that, the faith that my family and teammates had in me, made me better. I may not have always gained two hundred yards and certainly we didn't win every game, but they never shut me out after that first season. I wasn't going to let that happen again.[13]

In Principle #3, we will unpack adaptation, defined by author and entrepreneur Shane Parrish as the trait that "controls the sweet spot between reaction and prediction, providing an inherent ability to respond efficiently to a wide range of potential challenges, not just those that are known or anticipated. Adaptations are about being successful in your environment, so it becomes critical to define success. The point is that what matters is not the speed of adaptation, but what problems it helps you solve."[14]

ENDNOTES

1. Walter Payton with Don Yaeger, *Never Die Easy: The Autobiography of Walter Payton* (New York; Villard Books, 2000): 54.

2. Lisa Feldman Barrett, *Seven-and-a-Half Lessons about the Brain* (New York: HarperCollins, 2020).

3. David Eagleman and Johnathan Downer, *Brain and Behavior: A Cognitive Neuroscience Perspective,* 2nd Edition (London: Oxford University Press, 2023).

4. Andy Clark, *The Experience Machine: How Our Minds Predict and Shape Reality* (New York: Knopf Doubleday Publishing Group, 2023).

5. Umberto Castiello and Carlo Umiltà, "Size of the Attentional Focus and Efficiency of Processing." *Acta Psychologica* 73(3) (1990): 195-209. https://doi.org/10.1016/0001-6918(90)90022-8.

6. James J. Bell and James Hardy, "Effects of Intentional Focus on Skilled Performance in Golf." *Journal of Applied Sport Psychology* 21(2): 163-177. https//:doi.org/10.1080/10413200902795323.

7. Bell and Hardy, 170.

8. Áine MacNamara, Angela Button, and Dave Collins, "The Role of Psychological Characteristics in Facilitating the Pathway to Elite Performance: Part 2: Examining Environmental and Stage-Related Differences in Skills and Behaviors." *The Sport Psychologist* 24(1) (2010): 74–96.

9. Ayelet Fishbach, *Get It Done: Surprising Lessons from the Science of Motivation* (New York: Pan Macmillan, 2022).

10. Jared Weintraub, Kevin P. Nolan, and Aditi Rabindra Sachdev. "The Cognitive Control Model of Work-Related Flow." *Frontiers in Psychology* 14 (2023): https://doi.org/10.3389/fpsyg.2023.1174152.

11. Amishi P. Jha, *Peak Mind: Find Your Focus, Own Your Attention, Invest 12 Minutes a Day* (New York: HarperCollins, 2022).

12. Ibid.

13. Payton, 78.

14. Shane Parrish, *Clear Thinking: Turning Ordinary Moments into Extraordinary Results* (Toronto: Penguin Canada, 2023).

PRINCIPLE #3:

Adaptation

The capacity to adjust and improvise is arguably the single most critical human ability.

— *Will Smith*

Adaptation is not a foreign concept. We use this skill every day. We adapt by changing our plans to accommodate others. We adapt our attitude to suit an occasion. We adapt our level of thinking to the problem at hand. But in the world of high performance, adaptation means something a little different.

High performers know what skills—physical, mental, technical, or tactical—to use in what performance context, or what's known as "performative fit."[1] To reach the top, performers have to be able to adapt to a constantly changing performance environment.

In his book *The Great Mental Models*, Shane Parrish poses an apt definition of what it means for humans to adapt: "Adaptability is about recognizing when the way you have done things in the past is becoming less and less successful in a changing environment. It requires you to innovate, like mutations in the evolution time scale, to see if you can come up with ideas that will improve your chances of success." He goes on to specify that "adaptations are successful relative to their performance in a specific environment ... [adaptation] is both a noun and a verb. Adaptability controls the sweet spot between reaction and prediction, providing an inherent ability to respond efficiently to a wide range of potential challenges, not just those that are known or anticipated. Adaptations are about being successful in your environment, so it becomes critical to define success. The point is that what matters is not the speed of adaptation, but what problems it helps you solve."[2]

In the context of high performance, adaptation is about effectively adjusting and responding to the unfolding demands of the performance itself. Different from resilience, which we cover in Principle #5, adaptation is not about overcoming a known adversity or stress. Instead, adaptation is about staying in tune with what's required to prepare for the efficient use of our skills in the moment when it matters most.

A REMARKABLE STORY OF ADAPTATION

Jim Abbott was born with a disfigured right hand, which presented a unique (and perhaps for anyone else except for Jim aspiration-ending) challenge for a young man whose dream was to play major league baseball. Did I tell you he wanted to be a pitcher?

Next time you watch a baseball game, pay attention to way the pitcher prepares to deliver a pitch. They use their gloved hand to disguise the type of pitch and their other hand to throw the ball. The pitcher then sets up a defensive posture to field the ball if the hitter sends the ball in their direction. Pitchers play a unique role in that they initiate the play *and* participate as a fielder, whereas the rest of the team simply waits for the batter's response. A pitcher's ability to rapidly shift between initiating the play and responding to a screamer of a line drive is facilitated by having the use of two hands.

For Jim to succeed at initiating the play (throwing a pitch) and quickly shifting to defense, as well as prepare for delivering his pitches, he had to adapt. It began at a young age, where Jim would throw a ball against a wall and practice switching his glove, which was tucked under his arm, to his hand as quickly as possible. To increase the challenge, he would move closer to the wall, requiring him to increase the speed of his adaptation.

As Jim progressed through his baseball career, forcing himself to adapt to the speed of the ball of the wall paid off. Jim could bat one-handed, defend without needing to pitch, and of course, deliver as a high-caliber pitcher. He even played a short stint as a high-school quarterback and put up prolific statistics before deciding to stick with baseball.

Jim was drafted in the eighth round of the major league draft, which is pretty early on in the draft process. He enjoyed a successful ten-year career in the majors with the California Angels and New York Yankees and left a legacy as a person and performer for his ability to adapt to the circumstances and constraints of his performance.[3]

Part of what makes Jim unique is how he thought about his disability. He never used his physical limitation as an excuse or a reason to not be successful, and instead focused on his ability to adapt and perform with some of the best athletes in the world. In his book: *An Improbable Life*, Jim details how his relationship with his disability evolved when he told his daughter—who asked if he liked his "little hand"—"I do, honey. I like my little hand. I haven't always liked it. And it hasn't always been easy. But, it has taught me an important lesson, [which is] that life isn't easy and it isn't always fair. But, if we can make the most out of what we've been given, and find our own way of doing things, you wouldn't believe what can happen." He went on to say that there "was never just a focus on trying to bring attention to my situation, but there extremely was the idea of being the best pitcher I could be."[4]

Jim is an exemplar of what it means to adapt, and how changing our way of thinking can help us become the best we can be. Though overshadowed by the physical demonstration of overcoming his disability, Jim's psychological adaptation to his disability showcases what it means to be **psychologically flexible**. He quite literally changed his relationship with his own body, shifting it from a limitation to an inspiration. This chapter is about the tools we can use to facilitate that same shift within ourselves.

THE SCIENCE OF ADAPTABILITY

The Role of Psychological Flexibility in Adaptation

If there's one psychological framework and performance skill I make sure to teach to each athlete I work with, it's psychological flexibility. As we explored in Quality #4: Flexibility, at its core psychological flexibility is "the tendency to respond to situations in ways that facilitate valued goal pursuit."[5] The research behind psychological flexibility grew out of an attempt to identify core cognitive and behavioral processes that would allow people to respond in a healthy way to the daily stressors and challenges of life. Psychological flexibility is a predictor of a range of physical health outcomes, performance in sports, and even quality of life.[6]

When I coach I emphasize that psychological flexibility has two components, which are aligning our behavior with our values and not letting our thoughts or feelings derail us. Think about Jim Abbott. His goal was to pitch in the major leagues, and he never deviated an inch. He didn't give up, even when he didn't possess the same physical attributes as his role models and other professional players. He stayed dedicated to his craft and devoted to his dream, and learned to change his relationship to any self-limiting beliefs so that they wouldn't interfere with the pursuit of his goal.

This ability to stay doggedly persistent in pursuit of our values is special. It's what allows some of the all-time great visionaries in business to change the world, or what lets pro athletes go to work when nobody else is watching. Psychological flexibility is about putting in the work to become who you want to become. It's about understanding what you value, what your short-term goals are and how they link to those values, and what you can do today to get there. It's about seeing yourself as more than a sum of your experiences, learning to accept your emotions instead of resisting them so you can keep your eye on the prize, and treating thoughts as just passive experiences instead of literal truths. If you can put these skills together, you have a recipe for success in any performance, and over the long term as well.

Effective Adaptation and Elite Performance

We've touched on what psychological flexibility is in broad strokes. It's time to get into the components of psychological flexibility that facilitate effective adaptation in elite performance.

Component #1: Being Open

To be open means to be receptive to our internal experiences. At the elite level in sports, the performer doesn't spend much time or attention on how they're feeling or what they're thinking, unless their thinking or feeling needs a tune-up. They focus on (1) the demands of the task; (2) changes in the environment; and (3) changes in themselves.

When performance begins to deteriorate or fall off track, it often starts because of an external demand but is escalated by an internal demand. This thinking can quickly lead to feelings of tension or anxiety, and before we know it, our performance is off the rails. Think about the last time you were in a meeting and were called on unexpectedly. Chances are you started to search through your mind for the answer, while simultaneously sifting through internal dialogue suggesting "you should've been more prepared" or "you better get this right." Being open is about learning to let go of that internal dialogue, to accept the elevated arousal and anxiety that accompanies it, and to stay focused on finding the right answer.

The art of letting go of thinking happens through a process psychologists call "defusion." In the case of peak performers, defusion is about learning to let go of unhelpful dialogue, like "you better get this right," and to distance ourselves from the content of the thinking and the impact it has. Research shows that people who are able to decenter from their thinking are less reactive to what goes on in the mind and are better able to attend to what's happening in the moment.[7] As you know now, this is critical for high performance. You can't hit a fastball thinking about what you're having for dinner.

Being open also relates to our emotions. When we feel something, we have a few options: we can fight it, try to suppress it, or allow it to be. When we try to fight it, we usually make it worse. We feel sad about feeling sad, disappointed about feeling angry. When we try to suppress it, we might manage in the moment, but we hurt ourselves over the long term. What you don't deal with now almost always shows up later.

The psychologically flexible alternative is to allow it. That doesn't mean that you want to feel this way, but it means you're *willing* to feel it if it means you can keep on track toward meeting your goals. Think about the surgeon who makes a mistake in the operating room. They feel disappointed, frustrated, or angry. If they're *willing* to feel it, they can learn from it, and they won't make that mistake again. And, they won't be distracted trying to get rid of it or beat themselves up for feeling that way, only making it likely that a mistake is repeated. Being willing and open to feel what you feel frees you up to be present with your full experience of the world.

Being open means being able to adapt to the ebb and flow of thoughts and feelings that arise during a performance, yet remain attuned to the environment. Psychologically flexible and adaptive performers remain acutely aware of changes in the environment, which is the second component.

Component #2: Being Aware

An excellent performance begins with awareness. Awareness with respect to psychological flexibility is about (1) staying in the present moment, and (2) being able to experience yourself as bigger than your thinking, feeling, and physiology. Awareness allows you to take in your surroundings and then adapt to your environment accordingly.

Awareness can be compromised by a number of things, such as ruminating over past mistakes or thinking about future execution. Both of these are best reserved for the readiness phase of performance. Once the pitch, presentation, or game goes live, the best performers keep their attention grounded firmly in the here and now. The reason is if you're not paying attention to the present, you're going to miss the signals you need to do your best: how your audience is responding, how the opponent is moving, or even what slide you are sharing. Remaining aware of what's happening in the here and now is one of the simplest ways to instantly improve performance, and you can always draw upon this skill without any external requirement.

The second aspect of awareness, this sense that you are bigger than your inner experience, has been termed *self-as-context*. In essence, it means that you as a performer are able to identify with the part of yourself which contains thoughts, feelings, or physiology, and can clearly detect those times when these elements are not *the same as* the container. While this can seem like a complicated concept, most people have had some sort of transcendental experience that affirms the existence of this container-like state.

To make this even more concrete, think about all the identities you hold. To use myself as an example, I am a father, husband, friend, performance psychologist, coach, advisor, brother … and that's just what I can think of in fifteen seconds or so. I am not just one of those things, but all of them. I am more than any one identity.

Having the ability to see myself this way means that I can still find meaning and value in myself, even when things don't go my way. This is a concept most athletes I've worked with really have difficulty deploying. They're so committed to their identity as an athlete that any mistake or failure seems catastrophic. They're inflexible in how they think about themselves, which makes them unnecessarily hard on themselves after a poor performance.

We try to expand their sense of self by exploring their other identities, and by noticing that, when they have a difficult thought or feeling, they're both simultaneously feeling it *and* noticing that they're feeling it. You can't be the feeling and the container at the same time. That sense of awareness creates a little wiggle room for some space between stimulus and response.

In the context of peak performance, this state allows us to rise above discomfort and critical self-talk and continue to perform. You may not realize it, but if you've ever pushed yourself just a little bit further in a workout or a conversation when your mind was telling you to stop, you've accessed this state—you've separated your thinking from who you are and what you do. For top performers, the ability to access this transcendental mental state can help them better cope with difficulties and return to the task at hand.

PRINCIPLE #3: Adaptation

Component #3: Being Engaged

Being engaged is comprised of two processes: (1) a clear identification of values, and (2) alignment of behavior with those actions.

Engagement shows up during all phases of performance. Engagement is as much about what you do as how you do it. For example, you can choose to engage in practice by going all-out, using up all the energy you have (we talked about commitment in Principle #2). This level of commitment would be aligned around a personal value of "effort." Or you could just go through the motions in practice. That lesser commitment may be due to a lack of a personal value. Similarly, choosing to debrief can be done with thoughtfulness and deliberation, or as a check-the-box exercise ... or not done at all. The level of engagement is tied to personal values.

One of the beauties of sport is that performance itself is an opportunity to express our highest values. Performances showcase excellence, lay bare the work that has been done, and provide each athlete with an opportunity to express themselves within the rules of the game.

Such a high level of self-expression is not limited to sport, of course. If you've watched any of Taylor Swift's *Eras* tour, for example, you've seen a musician performing at the highest level, fully immersed in a state of self-expression unparalleled in the industry. And, this same engagement has undoubtedly shown up in people you've known in your own life.

On a recent trip I took to visit a venture capitalist in San Francisco, I got firsthand experience with one of the most engaged performers I've ever had the pleasure to meet. From the moment I met him face-to-face, his presence was palpable. He was fully present, clearly committed to his mission of changing the world's climate crisis, and full of love for the people in his network and team. In each discussion, he was able to tie back what he was doing on a daily basis—visiting with investors, founders, and team members—to the kind of organization he wants to create. And he even brought his family with him along for a trip across North America, an expression of his deep commitment to taking care of his loved ones. One day with a person like this is enough to shake your sense of how engaged you are and inspire you to make some changes.

ADAPTATION IN ACTION

Though the components that make up psychological flexibility may seem straightforward, putting them into regular practice to enhance our performance is not easy. Developing a state of psychological flexibility, like the other states we have discussed, takes practicing a core set of skills that allow us to execute. Fortunately, many of these skills are accessible at any moment, which means we can practice them both formally and informally, and perhaps more frequently than other skills in this book.

The Role of Values

We'll begin with values. For many sport psychology practitioners, the process of working with an individual performer actually begins entirely with the identification of a core set of values, which can guide the rest of the work.

A value by definition is something that is meaningful to you, and, importantly, brings a sense of vitality to your life. Your values should be the guiding principles in your life and performance, and provide a context for success. Think of success as aligning your actions with your values consistently over time. And remember, these values do not need to reflect who you are now. They should reflect the type of person and performer you want to become.

Coach's Corner: Identifying Values

There are several ways that we can identify values, so read through the following options and select the one that you think works best for you. Note that your values may or may not be context-dependent (you might value something at home differently than at work, for example) and that they are likely to change or evolve over time.

When I work with athletes or executives, one of the ways I start our process is by identifying values. My favorite way to do this is to ask them to imagine what they'd want their Hall-of-Fame bust to say about them. What kind of person were they? Why did they matter? Who did they serve? Answering these kinds of questions can give us a sense of clarity on what we're really doing the work for and what we hope to get out of it.

Use Reflection

Another tactic to use in adaptation is to reflect on the most impactful experiences of your life. Think about the moments you felt most connected to yourself and others, most energized, most present, or best about something you had done. Next, write down the qualities you brought to that particular moment. Perhaps you felt most connected when you expressed a deep caring for someone else, or you were most energized by seeing yourself get just a little bit better at a skill you'd been working on for some time. As you collect these moments, see if you can write down just one or two core characteristics that really resonate with you.

In a recent experience helping retired NFL players fully transition to life after the game, I had the opportunity to speak with one former pro about what kept him hooked on the game so long. He loved competing, connecting with his teammates in the locker room, and pushing himself to be better each day. The question to ease his retirement was not "Could we find new values now?" But instead, "How can we bring those values into your life post-game?" Having clarity on what moves you allows you to bring those qualities to bear in other aspects of your life and allows you to feel more connected in the process.

Most people find that they can group their values in clusters with some higher-order themes. The most important piece of these exercises is identifying what moves you, and being ready to put those values at the center of your life and performances.

Values and Committed Action

Committed action flows naturally from values identification. Once we know who we want to become and how we want to show up as a performer, we can start to align our actions around our values. The values become our guidepost, a way to check in with ourselves and ensure we are progressing. Exceptional performers choose the path that aligns with their values, even when it's challenging. For example, a performer who values excellent preparation might not *feel* like practicing the same speech again, but knows that to be authentic to themselves, spending even a little time reviewing and practicing aligns with who they want to be.

One simple way to put committed action into practice is to set goals. A lot has been made about the type of goal-setting that should be done (SMART goals, SMART-ER goals, SMART-EST goals …), but the method of goal-setting isn't nearly as important as just establishing a goal for yourself. You can do this with SMART goals, OKRs (objectives and key results), or other metrics.

What makes goals useful in the context of committed action is that they are tangible, measurable ways of ensuring alignment with our values. The values should dictate the goals we set, and the goals should be a simple way to make sure we're on the right track.

The most important piece of goal-setting is that the goal be specific enough to be enacted with small steps. If the goal seems daunting or nebulous, you haven't done enough work. The best athletes often set goals at the beginning of the season, which are micro-goals and macro-goals. For example, Super Bowl–winning wide receiver Odell Beckham Jr., after his 2022 victory, shared a photo of himself in front of the goal mirror he had made, with marks for specific performance metrics (like number of receptions or receiving yards) he had been aiming for that year. He had also set a goal to win the Super Bowl. His goals were specific so he could track his progress, and they likely aligned with a value many elite performers share in sport—excellence at their craft.

> **Committed Action: How Are You Showing Up?**
> Outside of goal-setting, committed action can give you a quick pulse check of how you are showing up during your performance. If your energy is low or you are disengaged and you catch yourself, simply ask what small step you can take right now that best aligns with the type of performer you want to be, and then challenge yourself to take that step. Taking the action is what's likely to change how we feel, not the other way around. Staying connected to our values in performance can help us ensure that, no matter the outcome, we can take pride in making a good effort and doing good work.

The Role of Defusion in Performance

Thinking is one of the fastest ways to disrupt elite sport performance. In fact, research suggests that even the best athletes in the world are vulnerable to having their performance disrupted under pressure by distracting thoughts.[8] If you don't believe thoughts could have so much of an impact, here's a quick way to illustrate. Try to explain to someone else how to walk. Literally explain each tiny action a person should take to walk. You'll quickly find that it's really, really hard. Not because we don't know how to walk, but because the act of walking has become so automatic that trying to describe it interferes with the movement itself. When this happens in a game, we call it having the "yips" or "choking." Essentially, our thinking disrupts what our body knows how to do.

The tricky part about managing our thoughts is that we do not have much control over what thoughts we have or when they show up. What we can control is how much we engage with those thoughts and how much those thoughts drive our behavior. We can choose what thoughts help or hurt, and work to negate the impact of unhelpful thoughts that interfere with our behavior. That's where defusion comes in.

Defusion is about minimizing the impact of unhelpful thinking on performance. To do that, we first need to get past a common fallacy about thinking that many people hold implicitly: that what we're thinking is inherently true, and thus needs to be listened to. Now for a quick demonstration.

Take a moment right now and, wherever you are, find a place to sit down. Sit with your feet on the ground, back straight, and in an alert position. Then, I want you to say the phrase, out loud, "I can't stand up," while simultaneously standing up. It's that simple. Take a second and do that a few times now. If you want to get really creative, you can add in "I can't sit down" while you sit back down between repetitions.

Silly as this exercise may sound, this simple act has helped countless of performers I've coached realize two critical things: how much credence they normally give to their thoughts and how much more control they have over their actions than they typically account for.

Now that we've established that baseline, there are a few things you can do to neutralize thoughts that interfere with your performance. Many of them might seem silly, but try to not let that thought interfere with giving them a shot. We've already explored one option by acting the opposite of our thoughts. Here are three more to get started.

Use Semantic Satiation to Neutralize Unhelpful Thoughts

Pick a single word or phrase that tends to interfere with your performance or changes your emotional or physiological state. For many performers, this might be "You're a failure" or "You suck." (It can be hard to be honest about how we talk to ourselves, but for the sake of this exercise, honesty is critical.)

Once you've identified your phrase, set a timer on your phone for thirty seconds. When you click start, simply repeat the word or phrase as many times as you can in thirty seconds. Try it now and come back when you're done.

If you're like most people, you just experienced semantic satiation, which is the technical term for what happens when we repeat a word so much that it loses its meaning. This exercise shows us in a tangible way that, at their core, words are really just strange sounds of letters mushed together that we've attached significant meaning to—the thoughts we have are real, but not necessarily true. This simple exercise can give you the freedom to let go of that difficult word or phrase, and not take it so seriously.[9]

Use Labeling to Neutralize Unhelpful Thoughts

The simple act of describing what is happening can put boundaries around unhelpful or limiting thoughts. In mindfulness meditation, this is called "labeling." Labeling works by creating distance between the core of the thought and the mind that created the thought. It is a strategy for quickly letting go of an unhelpful thought.

There are a few ways you can practice this tool. The first is to simply call out the unhelpful thought. "What am I thinking? This is garbage." When I am guilty of thinking unhelpful thoughts, I poke fun at myself to break the chain of self-criticism and see the words for what they are.

Labeling puts distance between our mind and the intensity of the thought. We now have some space to refocus and put our values back into practice and let them drive our next action. Research shows that the simple act of labeling is enough to lessen the visceral impact of the thought or feeling we're having.[10]

Use Writing to Neutralize Unhelpful Thoughts

Writing down self-critical thoughts externalizes them and allows the performer to really examine what they are saying to themselves. Some performers take it a step further and examine evidence that directly counteracts the thoughts they have. Both steps can be helpful in more objectively examining our realities and letting go of thoughts that hold us back.

The Role of Acceptance in Performance

Acceptance gets a bad rap. When people hear the word acceptance, they typically think of giving up and just letting life happen to them. Psychological flexibility requires acceptance of a different sort. It's an active state of choosing to be present with whatever experience you're having, *if there's nothing you can do to change it*. If defusion is about freeing up how performers work with difficult thoughts, acceptance is about freeing up how we work with difficult emotions.

There is a remarkable amount of our experience we can do almost nothing about. We can't always control what we think, we can't control what our bosses or friends say or do, we can't control the traffic around us—but all of these things directly impact how we feel. Acceptance is about allowing those experiences to unfold as they are, without resisting them. If there is a circumstance you can do something about, great! Do it! If not, the next best move is to allow yourself to experience it.

The simplest way to begin practicing acceptance is by homing in on our breathing and imagining that we can breathe directly into the discomfort we are experiencing. Most emotions have a physical signature—a racing heart, a pain in the chest, a feeling in the pit of the stomach—so find that physical signature and imagine you can breathe directly into it. Allow the experience to be there and allow yourself to experience it fully, without resistance.

Once you've allowed yourself time with the difficult emotion and sensation, the next best step is to reorient to the values. Choose a behavior that fits the next best action in your circumstance that aligns with your values and get started. Often times, just getting started is enough to lessen the emotional intensity and use that energy for good.

Present Moment Focus & Self-as-Context

Present moment focus and self-as-context can be practiced together with one exercise—mindfulness. In fact, mindfulness helps with all of these processes, but can be especially helpful for training our mind to stay focused on the present moment and help us practice noticing how our thoughts, feelings, and physical sensations exist within us but aren't the same as us. As you can probably see, being present and seeing ourselves as more than the sum of our internal experiences lends itself nicely to both acceptance and defusion. And the other advantage of mindfulness practice, when done with the breath, is that the breath can serve as an anchor during performances that we can train ourselves to return to. In that moment, we can restore our presence and redirect our attention to the performance task at hand.

* * *

With the tactics we have described, we are positioned to adapt to nearly anything that arises during performance. If resilience helps us deal with setbacks, adaptability helps us effectively execute during the constant unfolding and evolving demands of elite performance. By developing their psychological flexibility, top performers are armed to manage their psychological and physiological states with a range of skills that allow them to stay expertly attuned to the performance at hand. They can direct attention to the skills they need to succeed in any specific situation, and optimally adapt and perform.

THE INCREDIBLE US PARAJUMPERS

It's hard for many of us to even *think* about jumping from a plane. Now imagine jumping from one feared situation to an even deadlier situation—one wherein you have to defuse a live bomb.

This was the exact dynamic I was brought in to help with when I worked with Parajumpers at Davis-Monthan Air Force Base in Tucson, Arizona. These highly trained, tactically proficient professionals were responsible for some of the most intense performances in the military, and one of their mine jobs was to help in the defusion of improvised explosive devices, or IEDs.

Both jumping from a plane and defusing a live bomb require incredible psychological flexibility. The jump from a plane alone is enough to raise your heart rate, and failing to be present with any aspect of that performance—distracted by thoughts, taken out of the moment by emotion—is a recipe for disaster. Then, as soon as that ends, they'd have to quickly adapt and switch their attention to the intense process of defusing an explosive. One wrong move was literally the difference between life and death.

To train for that, we used mindfulness to redirect attention. I taught them how to let go of their unhelpful thoughts, like thoughts about a mistake during the jump or fears about not being there for their family. And we covered *why* they were doing this work—what are their values and what drives their daily action? How do they want to be remembered?

As we built a psychologically flexible foundation, the fear of jumping out of a plane or defusing a bomb didn't go away, but the relationship to the fear was transformed. It was a sign that performance was going *right*, not that something would go wrong.

***

From being adaptable we will turn to how you optimize your energy. When high performers talk about poise, calming their nerves, or performing under pressure, they're typically talking about managing their thoughts, feelings, and physiology in the biggest moments. The truth is, nerves are a normal and even helpful part of performance, if we can learn to think about them correctly. Even the highest-caliber athlete is nervous with the game on the line, and managing that nervousness effectively can be a key to success. The performer who can most quickly optimize their energy—using their thinking, feeling, and physiology to facilitate performance, rather than inhibit it—is likely to increase their odds of winning.

When you need to be your best, the energy you are going to release has to meet the demands of the performance. But releasing too much too soon may result in a failing performance. What is the secret that elite performers have to manage this precious resource?

ENDNOTES

1. Joe Higgins, "Why Roger Federer Is a GOAT: An Account of Sporting Genius." *Journal of the Philosophy of Sport* 45(3) (2018): 296-317.

2. Shane Parrish and Rhiannon Beaubien, *The Great Mental Models, Volume 1: General Thinking Concepts* (New York: Penguin, 2024): 138-139.

3. Jim Abbott and Tim Brown, *Imperfect: An Improbable Life* (New York: Ballantine Books, 2013): 18-19.

4. Peter J. Wallner, "How Jim Abbott Settled His Insecurity over Deformed Hand to Become a Successful Big League Pitcher." Mlive (May 2, 2012). https://www.mlive.com/sports/grand-rapids/2012/05/how_jim_abbott_settled_his_ins.html.

5. James D. Doorley, Fallon R. Goodman, Kerry C. Kelso, and Todd B. Kashdan. "Psychological Flexibility: What We Know, What We Do Not Know, and What We Think We Know." *Social and Personality Psychology Compass* 14(12) (2020): 1-11.

6. Todd B. Kashdan and Jonathan Rottenberg, "Psychological Flexibility as a Fundamental Aspect of Health." *Clinical Psychology Review* 30(7) (2010): 865-878.

7. Amit Bernstein, Yuval Hadash, and David M. Fresco, "Metacognitive Processes Model of Decentering: Emerging Methods and Insights." *Current Opinion in Psychology* 28 (2019): 245-251.

8. Leo J. Roberts, Mervyn S. Jackson, and Ian H. Grundy, "Choking under Pressure: Illuminating the Role of Distraction and Self-Focus." *International Review of Sport and Exercise Psychology* 12(1) (2019): 49-69.

9. Ibid.

10. Jared B. Torre and Matthew D. Lieberman, "Putting Feelings into Words: Affect Labeling as Implicit Emotion Regulation." *Emotion Review* 10(2) (2018): 116-124. https://doi.org/10.1177/1754073917742706.

PRINCIPLE #4:

Energy Optimization

I try to stay as calm as possible and focus on one day at a time, but when reality sets in, I feel everything: anxiety, excitement, nerves, pressure, and joy.

— *Shawn Johnson, US Olympic Gymnast*

Backstage, hearing thousands scream in anticipation, Shawn Mendes gathers his team in a huddle. For any performer, performing in front of a sellout crowd of fifty thousand cheering fans would trigger anxiety and exhilaration (thankfully, fans also can activate the *social facilitation effect*, which helps us perform better in front of others). For Shawn on this particular night, the pressure has reached another level. The show is his first stadium show—and it's in his hometown, Toronto.

The first thing he lets the team know is how he is feeling. "I don't have the most incredible words to say right now, because my heart is racing." He's describing a typical experience for any performer—elevated arousal. "I'm the first to say that I don't even know if I should be here right now," he continues. Shawn's team members feel his energy, which in turn is amping up their own nervous energy. He's also expressing humility and acknowledging that what he's about to do—with their help—is very challenging.

In the blink of an eye, Shawn then masterfully changes his relationship with his arousal experience. He starts to talk about how this performance is "special." And he's not exaggerating or hyperbolic because he's home. He's talking about the opportunity to perform, to impact the crowd, to do something rare. He talks about everyone deserving to be present for the opportunity and letting "joy overcome [them]."

What's happened here? He's gone from feeling nervous and acknowledging self-doubt, which his team feels too, to making his team feel deserving of being on stage. He's turned their communal racing hearts into a shared team experience that's going to be one of a kind. As the huddle breaks, the team aligns with a cheer that signals their readiness—"Let's go!" The team closes the huddle with two words: "awesome energy."

As a high performer, Shawn Mendes understands how important it is to stay regulated—the act of optimizing your energy to help you perform at your peak. In the Netflix documentary *In Wonder*, he details how he feels when he walks on stage. He makes reference to his self-talk that heightens his arousal and the impact of his elevated arousal on his performance (his first note is typically flat). As he experiences the consequences of being over-aroused, he coaches himself into his optimal performance zone. He reminds himself that he loves music, encourages himself to let go, and to "just do this."

It's common for performers to experience difficulty delivering in big moments. Arousal is a key part of any performance. Mendes tells his team, "As a performer, you get very nervous; sometimes you freak out and things can become a lot for you." But rather than let the nerves dictate how well or not he performs, he uses the nerves as fuel. "If you get nervous it means you care, and I care about nothing more in the world than you guys, so that's why my hands shake." In one sentence, Mendes demonstrates one of the most powerful skills we have for regulating our energy—*reframing*.

While there are many dimensions to Shawn's performance, his ability to get into the flow of his performance so capably hinges on his ability to manage his energy. He's acutely aware of the effects of arousal on his performance. Like many elite performers, he has identified a set of skills that enable him to deliver a seemingly effortless and painless performance.

Here's a quick synopsis of the tools Shawn has used to get himself ready to perform. In engaging in reframing, he changes his appraisal of a racing heart from being caused by anxiety to an acknowledgment that something special is happening. That simple act of changing how he perceives an internal sensation changes the experience of the performance from being a threat to a challenge, which facilitates optimal performance.

A second strategy Shawn uses is social connection. Humans have evolved to be highly social creatures. We co-regulate one another's energy efficiency.[1] In other words, we help each other manage our energy. Although Shawn's team likely doesn't realize just how much their presence and support help him (and Shawn may not even fully appreciate it), his ability to create a sense of camaraderie (and thus connection) lets his team know he feels cared about—that he and the team are part of a community bigger than themselves.

Shawn leverages the power of self-talk to help him walk onto the stage with confidence. The team breaks the huddle with "Let's go!" This energy-pumping phrase signals that it's time to perform. It's a simple, powerful tool called motivational self-talk that brings everyone into the moment. Their hard work rehearsing and preparing is now in the limelight.

Shawn's masterclass on regulation demonstrates the wide variety of influences on arousal and the skills he deploys to facilitate peak performance. Elite performers adopt and adapt a host of energy management skills that allow them to wow their audience. Some performers, like Beyonce and Kobe Bryant, even adopt alter egos to fuel their performance. It's an energy management tactic that allows them to cope with pressure.

Though the combination of skills that exceptional performers use to manage their nerves and use their energy for good may vary, they understand that regulation is about finding the balance between the energy needed to perform and the poise and presence to deliver under pressure. As our example with Shawn Mendes also illustrates, finding this balance involves *down-regulating*. There's a general consensus that, while skills can be developed to increase arousal, it's much more common to experience over-arousal.

For us to be our best when it matters most, we have to learn to regulate our actions, thoughts, feelings, and physiology. We'll turn our attention there next, but before we do so, there's one important distinction to make: **regulation is not the same thing as controlling.**[2] The reality is that our thoughts, feelings, and physiology are influenced by a number of factors outside of our control, including our immediate physical and social environments. Rather than focusing on controlling or changing our thoughts, feelings, or physiology, performers change *the relationship* they have with each of these aspects by doing things like calling nerves "a sign you care." It's not the thought that counts—it's how you relate to the thought that makes the difference.

THE SCIENCE OF ENERGY MANAGEMENT

When high performers talk about poise, calming their nerves, or performing under pressure, they're typically talking about managing their thoughts, feelings, and physiology in the biggest moments. The truth is, nerves are a normal and even helpful part of performance, if we can learn to think about them correctly. Even the highest-caliber athlete is nervous with the game on the line, and managing that nervousness effectively can be a key to success. The performer who can most quickly optimize their energy—using their thinking, feeling, and physiology to facilitate performance, rather than inhibit it—is likely to increase their odds of winning.

In my work with Olympic athletes, the nerves before the games rise to an all-time high. Olympians are given one shot every four years to show what they're made of, and the circumstances surrounding the Olympic Games are unlike almost any other they've experienced. The living conditions are novel, the family experience is novel, and the television presence is novel.

Research supports the idea that Olympians' main concern is managing pressure and the energy that goes along with it.[3] Olympians are forced to deal with a number of factors beyond their control and have just one shot to deliver their best (though they may have multiple trials that they have to do well in to get that one shot). In these high-stakes situations, nothing can derail a performance faster than mismanaged energy.

As you might expect, all of this uncertainty, novelty, and pressure are inimical to staying cool, calm, and collected. That's why one of the first things I do in working with Olympic athletes is to identify what ramps up their energy past a point where it's no longer helpful, and then I work with them to develop skills to cope and refocus. We don't want them using their energy up before the performance. We want them squarely in the zone for go-time.

Energy Optimization and Efficiency

The scientific terminology for energy management or energy optimization is *regulation*. Regulation is about matching our internal state—our thinking, feeling, and physiology— to the demands of the performance. Some performances, like chess, don't require an elevated heart rate or a physical warmup, but rather a calm, poised demeanor. Other types of performance require a great deal of energy, like climbing up the face of a rock without a rope, which must be carefully controlled and managed over a long period of time. And still others require a massive burst of energy for a remarkably short period of time, like fewer than ten seconds to complete a hundred-meter dash.

I use the term *energy efficiency* throughout this chapter to describe the different regulation strategies that allow us to channel our energy most effectively. Both our physiological arousal and emotional arousal can be thought of as energy. Psychologists have extensively explored "arousal regulation" and "emotion regulation," but the complex interplay between our thinking, feeling, and physiology can make it challenging to tease apart what exactly a high performer needs to regulate these dimensions of energy. Let's explore these now.

Performers have three dials to adjust to optimize energy efficiency: (1) thinking, (2) feeling, and (3) physiology. Delivering our best when it matters most requires recognizing managing our thoughts, feelings, and physiology under the greatest of pressures and brightest of lights. Each of these components impacts one another in a complex way. Understanding our thinking, feeling, and physiology in the context of performance can give us greater control and facilitate high performance.

What we're trying to find by turning these dials is what's called our "individual zone of optimal functioning," or IZOF.[4] You have your own version of the Goldilocks principle for your performance. You don't want to be too hot or too cold, but just right. Finding your individual zone of optimal performance means finding the right balance of your energy—not too hot, not too cold—to deliver your best performance.

The Role of Thinking in Energy Management

The way we think about a performance, interpret a feeling, or assess our physiology has a huge impact on how we approach performing under pressure. Reflect on how Shawn Mendes prepared for his performance. At first, he experienced a threat mindset, which instills the belief we can't do something. Then through positive self-talk he transformed the threat mindset into a challenge mindset, which instills the belief we can handle the pressure. We are able to persist in the face of adversity and as such increase our energy. A threat mindset typically leads to withdrawal at the first sign of failure and a reduction of effort. It's hard to imagine a musician leaving the stage because they hit one bad note, which would be a result of a threat mindset.

Focusing our thinking by setting a new goal or attending to an important aspect of the performance is meaningful for energy efficiency. In Shawn's case, it may be switching up his set list to regulate his energy. For a team leader, it might be switching up priorities after reading the energy level of the team.

At times our thoughts can take us off task and waste our energy. Who hasn't questioned their success in delivering a public speech? Will the audience care about what I have to say? What if I make a mistake? Am I connecting with my audience? This type of thinking has to be reined in to deliver an expected result.

In sum, thinking, like the other two dials, can be a performance facilitator or debilitator. It plays a critical role in how we make sense of feeling and physiology, and guides our actions.

The Role of Feeling in Energy Management

A feeling is simply how we categorize what we're experiencing inside now based on current circumstances and past experience. For example, if we've often described ourselves as "overwhelmed" in a moment of pressure, we're likely to attribute our racing heart or frantic thinking to exactly that sensation. We do, however, have some alternatives. We could choose to categorize this experience as excitement, care, or even confidence.

This isn't about some old-school notion of "emotion versus logic," either. You're *always* feeling something.[5] The key, then, is to be able to identify what you're feeling and to shift the feelings to a place that works for you. We'll cover some tools you can use to shift your feelings later, but for now it's important to recognize that your feelings are a critical part of any peak performance, whether it's reading a jury in a courtroom or managing a team in the locker room. Emotion is foundational to what it means to be a real, high-performing human being.

The Role of Physiology in Energy Management

In order to perform, our body has to mobilize resources that allow us to deploy our practiced skills in the moment. This mobilization can lead to physiological changes like an increased heartbeat, clammy hands, and quickened breathing. Peak performance is about finding the optimal physiology to execute our skills as efficiently as possible. Too much physiological arousal interferes with execution. Not enough arousal, and we can't get off the bench and into the game.

Our physiology often operates just below our consciousness, and for good reason. If we were constantly aware of things like our heart rate or breathing, we'd essentially short circuit—it would be too much for our brain to process. That short-circuiting is what most performers experience when they step onto the big stage. They become more aware of things that they ordinarily don't have to mind, and suddenly, their focus is misdirected and they feel out of control. Learning to get our physiology back into a range that we're comfortable with and that enhances our performance, then, is mission critical for a great performance in difficult circumstances.

The Three Dials in Action

High performers understand that better monitoring and managing each of these dimensions of our internal experience increases our chances of peaking. Though we've looked at these elements independently to illustrate how they factor in to peak performance, they all work in synchronicity to influence our energy efficiency.

Each of us constantly engages with our patterns of thinking, feeling, and physiology, though we're often unaware of how they are impacting our performance in a given moment and sometimes even unaware that they're happening at all. For example, the average person thinks about seventy thousand thoughts per day, most of which happen outside conscious awareness.[6] Similarly, our body is constantly in a state of "feeling"—a combination of what scientists call "affect," or what we normally think of as mood, and our bodily sensations and physiology, like our heart rate and breathing. Our thinking, feeling, and physiology interact and influence and guide performance.

One of the greatest professional athletes of all time, Kobe Bryant, illustrates this point perfectly. In his book, *The Mamba Mentality: How I Play*, Kobe says, "The game is full of ebbs and flows—the good, the bad, and everything in between. With all that was going on around me, I had to figure out how to steel my mind and keep calm and centered. That's not to say my emotions didn't spike or drop here or there, but I was aware enough to recalibrate and bring them back level before things spiraled. I could do that in a way others couldn't, and that was really key for me."[7] The ability to meet the moment came down to optimizing his energy efficiency, directing his thinking, feeling and physiology to allow him to consistently deliver at his best. Of course, this level of self-mastery led to one of the most prolific careers in professional sports history. Kobe Bryant was an incredibly physically gifted athlete, and he also intimately understood and worked to master his regulation skills to help him deliver in the biggest moments. He knew that his physical abilities would help him compete in the NBA, but his competitive edge came from "recalibrating" in a way that others could not match.

The simplest way to think about the possible range of energy efficiency is known in performance psychology as the Yerkes–Dodson Law (or the "inverted U"), referred to earlier in Principle #1: Preparation.[8] What the inverted U teaches us is that there's a point where our physiology, thinking, and feeling are positioned to help us perform our best when it matters most. Our sweet spot is at the top of the inverted U, where it feels neither comfortable nor uncomfortable, but simply "right." To the left of that sweet spot, we're not using energy efficiently enough, and we are all intimately familiar with what it's like to be to the right of that sweet spot, where we have too much energy to effectively perform.

As I mentioned in Principle #1: Preparation, the brain's primary mechanism of action is predicting. In the case of regulation, energy efficiency really means the optimal predicting of energy needs given the circumstances of the performance. Framed this way, being under- or over-aroused happens because the brain miscalculates the energy needs in the moment. These predictions are based on our current physiology, past experience, and our current environment, including our thinking and our affect. The best performers train their brain to issue the most accurate predictions possible over time—by seeking out new experiences, practicing psychological skills, watching others, and more—leading to a better-managed state of energy in the biggest moments.[9]

Our thinking, feeling, and physiology are all a part of this energy efficiency equation. The interconnectedness of these processes means that managing to change just one of them can cascade changes to the others. In other words, we can use our thinking to change our feeling or physiology, change our physiology to change our thinking or feeling, or any other combination thereof. With a wider range of available places to intervene, we have a broader repertoire we can draw from to counteract any potential pitfalls. This broader range includes managing the current moment as well as engaging in longer-term strategies to optimize our energy efficiency.

A Comment on Long-Term Regulation

Before getting into skills for the moment, it's important to note that regulation can also happen on a longer time scale. In many ways, the pandemic that began in March of 2020 and will remain with us in different variants is one big exercise in regulation. To illustrate the point on a massive scale, organizational psychologist Adam Grant penned a prescient essay on what he termed a "boring apocalypse" in describing the onslaught of the Omicron variant of SARS-CoV-2. In the piece, Dr. Grant argues that the constant flood of information and frequent updates from news outlets on the tragic consequences of the pandemic will ultimately lead to a populous that appears to stop caring and be numbed to the new realities of a more contagious variant.[10]

This apparent numbness and lack of care, in actuality, is a normal response to repeated exposure to feared stimuli or situations. In essence, the more we come in to contact with something, the less scary we determine it to be as we learn about the regularities of the stimulus or situation and get better at assessing the real probabilities of adverse outcomes for ourselves.

Psychologists could have anticipated such an outcome—the idea of exposing people to a feared stimulus or situation and teaching them how to effectively moderate their response in the confrontation of such a stimulus is the cornerstone of many evidence-based therapies, and is one of the most strongly supported principles of change in the science itself. Facing your fears really does work, if you do it enough.

THE SCIENCE APPLIED

I've seen how poise can play out as a performance enhancer firsthand. In Tucson, Arizona, while serving as a sport psychologist, I had the privilege of consulting with an operational psychologist for the US Air Force and bringing performance psychology skills to the existing magnificent skill set of an elite Parajumper unit trained to defuse improvised explosive devices (IEDs). Not your typical performance, this was a test of poise with the ultimate consequence—life or death.

During my first meeting with this group, it became clear just how important staying well-regulated was to their mission. Optimizing their energy efficiency—both their physiological arousal and their emotional response—was just as important as their preparation, as the preparation could be squandered by a rushed decision or sweaty palms, with dire consequences. These performers had to be aroused enough to run, jump, and defend one another, and yet calm enough to manipulate tiny wires traced to explosives. High performance truly required finding optimal energy efficiency.

The start of our work together focused on what I often consider the first step of efficient energy use: deconstruction. In this case, deconstruction is about breaking down the whole experience into its component parts. For example, instead of working on "managing anxiety," we talked about "managing a racing heart," "managing a racing mind," and the other individual elements that make up the experience of anxiety. The simple act of deconstruction can make the experience of optimizing energy efficiency more effective.

We then identified and implemented specific strategies for each of these component parts. For the racing heart, we introduced breathing techniques like box breathing, a basic, balanced, and controlled breathing pattern that steadies the mind (see Principle #1: Preparation). For the racing mind, we introduced mindfulness meditation (see Principle #2: Immersion). For the (very real) fear of threat, we introduced cognitive reframing. Collectively, we helped them to develop an arsenal of techniques to be deployed at a moment's notice. With more practice, these already immensely skilled professionals felt increased confidence in their ability to use the skills and be their best when it mattered most.

Coach's Corner: Short-Term Strategies to Perform in the Moment

For many of the airmen, the strategies that were most important were those they could deploy on a moment's notice to tackle their specific thinking, feeling, and physiology. There is no "one-size-fits-all" approach to energy management. Psychologists know that the most effective strategies are those that are the best fit between situational demands and the strategy chosen.[11] The best way to optimize energy efficiency is to choose the strategy that works for you, given the challenge you're facing.

Adopt a Problem-Focused Strategy to Avoid Energy Depletion

The most significant finding relevant to the categories of energy management strategies is that a problem-focused strategy, which attempts to resolve the situation causing the unhelpful thinking, feeling, or physiology, is the most effective type of strategy.[12] There is an arsenal of tactics we can use to attack problems and make sure energy is used wisely.

Situation Modification

Situation modification involves taking direct action to change the situation giving rise to your unhelpful energy. For an athlete, this might mean changing the player you are guarding to make the challenge more manageable. For a team leader, this might mean insisting that cameras are turned on during a Zoom presentation so that you can better gauge reactions to a presentation.

For the parent, this might mean leaving the room for a moment so you don't say something you don't mean to your child.

Modifying our situation is arguably the most impactful thing we can do to change our behavior. Research consistently demonstrates the impact of the environment on our behavior, because so much of what we do is cued by what's around us.[13] Changing the situation has a dual benefit or altering the current problem and introducing a new circumstance that can better match your desired end state. Of course, you can't always modify the situation by leaving, but you can usually find something in your environment you can change to reduce the pressure and get back on track.

Reframing

As we saw in the Shawn Mendes example, reframing is the tactic whereby we name our thinking, feeling, and physiology whatever we like. This is why changing language from "nervous" to "excited" works. We've reframed (also known as recategorized) negative or inhibiting thoughts and feelings to positive thoughts and feelings to create the energy we need to facilitate and enhance performance.

Reframing has a host of other benefits as well. If we categorize an emotion as something harmful, like anxiety, we tend to elicit one set of responses from ourselves designed to reduce that anxiety or get rid of it altogether. But if we frame the same sensations as excitement, our goal shifts from getting rid of it to embracing and enjoying it. Though the physiological signatures of anxiety and excitement are the same, the framing of the emotion makes a big difference in how we actually experience it.

Take an NBA player at the free-throw line, with the game on the line. There are a few ways to think about this: as a chance to win the game, a chance to lose the game, a chance to be the hero, or a chance to let teammates down. In a pressure-packed moment like this, the athlete would have every right to call their feeling "nervousness." The only problem with that naming is the downstream negative effects it may have on performance: increased tension in the body, distracting thoughts, and an escalated heart rate.

In my work with NBA players in situations just like this, one of the first things we do is switch that framing from nervousness to "opportunity" or "determination." The underlying physiology is the same, but changing the category changes the way the brain responds. We "reframe" nervousness into something more useful, and the body is prepared to execute fluidly, focused, and collected. With conditions like this, the chance of sinking the game-winning shot go up exponentially.

Breathing

The mind and body are intimately connected. One simple way to more efficiently optimize your energy is to optimize your breathing. Different forms of patterned and controlled breathing can help us practice sustaining attention and modulating our responses under stress. For example, box breathing (maintaining the same steady rate of breathing in and breathing out) can help us re-center and better use our energy.

Data show that a regular breathwork practice can improve control of our arousal.[14] The breath is a shortcut to a lot of our internal sensations, and as we learn to control it, we feel a greater sense of mastery over the arousal we experience. That's why breathwork is one of the first tools I teach my athletes. It boosts confidence, is an actionable step they can take, and gives them control over one of the things most likely to derail a top performance.

Attentional Deployment

Oftentimes the thinking, feeling, and physiology tip to the right and become overwhelming when we turn our attention inward and assess our internal signals. For example, the performer giving a sales pitch might become overwhelmed when they notice their heart racing, and begin to question why their heart is racing in the first place. In this instance, it can be helpful to catch ourselves and redirect attention back to the task at hand. In most cases of peak performance, high performers find it most beneficial to stay focused on the environment and what is happening outside the body to facilitate optimal energy efficiency. For the same sales performer, it might mean refocusing on the reaction of the audience and staying attentive to how the message is being received.

Break the Problem Down

Energy is used unwisely when we try to solve one big problem. Let's look at an example. A swimmer, known for her consistent high performance, begins to struggle in competition. One way to deal with this would be to break her experience down into its component parts, asking her to observe and describe each part.

When it's broken down, the athlete can then identify strategies to use to address that specific situation, rather than the potentially overwhelming problem of poor performance.

A bonus to the process of breaking it down is that it tends to de-escalate the experience and depersonalize it. We gain some sense of distance from it, and that distance changes our relationship to it. Seeing it more clearly enables us to choose how to respond, if we choose to respond at all.

Move Your Body

The simplest thing we can do when we have mismanaged our energy is move our body and use that energy to bring ourselves back into balance.[15] Essentially, we've generated extra energy that we need to use, and movement is an efficient way to use that energy. This might be as simple as using our hands more when speaking to an audience or engaging in a quick bout of push-ups to pump ourselves up.

The Feared Stimulus Tactic

Applied to a performance setting, performance psychologists know that exposing people to a feared stimulus in a structured way can reduce the heightened arousal and fear response associated with that stimulus.[16] As the brain learns the statistical patterns associated with the stimulus, it can more easily predict what the stimulus means and thus how to respond. When managed correctly, this type of exposure can be thought of as an exercise in energy efficiency. High performers willingly expose themselves to a stressful circumstance or stimulus, learn to manage it, and then repeat. Over time, that original stressful circumstance will elicit a milder response, and using energy in the moment, should that circumstance arise, becomes easier. This is exactly what Alex Honnold did to prepare for El Capitan.

I apply this tactic regularly in my work with athletes returning from injury. An injury, which could potentially be career-ending, is an athlete's greatest fear. Once they've had an injury, the athlete will fear the same thing happening again. In these instances, athletes tend to over-index their attention on the injured body part and, as a result, compensate physically in a way that, ironically, increases the chance of re-injury.

To make this tactic work in these circumstances, we have to gradually expose the athlete to the activity they fear. Afterward, we process the experience in an act of consolidating new learning. This enables the athlete to consciously process that there's less to be afraid of than they feared. By repeating this tactic over time, the fear of re-injury is diminished because the path of recovery leads to pre-injury level of play.

A Final Note on the Foundations of Energy Efficiency

Top performers can engage other, more routine strategies that can help them optimize their energy efficiency both in the moment and outside performance. Like most elements of high performance, these

> tactics are not complicated, but what separates the best from the rest is consistent practice and use over time.
>
> Effective energy management starts with adequate sleep, nutrition, and hydration. Establishing a good baseline of energy is critical for making sure that performers can use their energy most efficiently. Simply put, managing energy is much more challenging when we're underfed and overtired.

The best performers find a way to optimize their energy efficiency. Readiness allows a performer to walk on stage with the necessary training and skills to deliver. Optimizing energy efficiency allows the performer to stay on task, balancing the demands of the performance with the necessary techniques, tactics, and strategies to meet the moment. The best performers are those that match their energy efficiency strategies to the situational demands, ensuring that they are performing at their peak. These strategies can help a high performer find that peak more readily and be their best when it matters most.

THE OPERATING THEATER

If you think running a marathon is tough, you should imagine doing an eight-hour surgery.

In my work with physicians, it's not uncommon for them to maintain just one position for an unusually long time, concentrating on their patient while addressing the target of their work, like a tumor or a bleed. Operating in these conditions is the ultimate act of energy efficiency, and that's before you layer on the emotional aspects that can sometimes accompany surgeries like traumatic wounds or injured children.

The process of managing energy during the surgery starts before the surgeon scrubs in. They review the charts and set a goal for the surgery, guiding their focus and attention, and putting a frame around the performance that determines success. This frame serves as a point of reference they can use to determine if they're on track or not.

Though the surgery may be routine, the best surgeons still experience a surge of adrenaline, a sign that they're about to do something significant. To control and channel that energy effectively, they can engage in breathwork and motivational self-talk, each of which helps them steel their nerves and guide energy toward action.

As the surgery starts, it becomes a matter of staying present and not over-reacting to the inevitable hiccups that accompany seeing parts of the body that imaging can't quite pick up. For eight hours, they must aim to stick in the zone, not so under-aroused that they're bored and lose focus, and not so over-aroused that they can't concentrate and execute.

If a problem arises, they deploy problem-focused coping strategies. An unanticipated internal bleed leads to modifying the situation, perhaps changing course altogether and resolving a more urgent issue. They don't throw their hands up and wonder why this is happening, but are able to stay intent on resolving what's on hand. If they make a mistake, however small, they let it go, deploying their attention more effectively back to the task at hand. If there's a moment of nerves or heightened arousal, it's reframed as a sign of care and concern, or passion for what they do.

These tools, deployed at the right time, allow them to maintain the stamina they need to stay hunched over, head down for hours on end. Without the ability to stay in their IZOF, these physicians would quit early, lose momentum, or overdo it too soon. It's an act of mastery of energy to perform for that long.

* * *

In the next chapter, we'll discuss the last principle, which is resilience. Regardless of how well we've prepared or how optimized we are, it's inevitable that we'll be confronted with something that we have to respond to effectively to be our best when it matters most. Adversity comes in many forms. There are things we cannot prepare for, such as last-minute changes and other circumstances that are beyond our control. These elements are inherent in high performance and are what make all performances odd-based events. Resilience is the state that allows us to return to top form after being challenged.

ENDNOTES

1. Lisa Feldman Barrett, *Seven-and-a-Half Lessons about the Brain* (New York: Houghton Mifflin, 2020): 83-85.

2. Michael Inzlicht, Kaitlyn M. Werner, Julia L. Briskin, and Brent W. Roberts, "Integrating Models of Self-Regulation." *Annual Review of Psychology* 72(1) (2021): 319-345. https://doi.org/10.1146/annurev-psych-072220-104358.

3. Rachel Arnold and Mustafa Sarkar, "Preparing Athletes and Teams for the Olympic Games: Experiences and Lessons Learned from the World's Best Sport Psychologists." *International Journal of Sport and Exercise Psychology* 13(1) (2015): 4-20. https://doi.org/10.1080/1612197X.2014.932827.

4. Yuri L. Hanin, "Emotions and Athletic Performance: Individual Zones of Optimal Functioning Model." In D. Smith and M. Bar-Eli (Eds.), *Essential Readings in Sport and Exercise Psychology* (London, Human Kinetics, 2007): 55-73.

5. Barrett, *Seven-and-a-Half Lessons about the Brain*, 79-81.

6. "Brain Facts." Healthy Brains by Cleveland Clinic (May 11, 2020). https://healthybrains.org/brain-facts/.

7. Kobe Bryant, *The Mamba Mentality: How I Play* (New York: Farrar, Straus and Giroux, 2018).

8. R.M. Yerkes and J.D. Dodson, "The Relationship of Strength of Stimulus to Rapidity of Habit Formation." *Journal of Comparative Neurology and Psychology* 18 (1908): 459-482.

9. Barrett, *Seven-and-a-Half Lessons about the Brain*, 79-81.

10. Adam Grant, "We're Living Through the Boring Apocalypse." *The New York Times* (December 10, 2021).

11. George A. Bonnano and Charles L. Burton, "Regulatory Flexibility: An Individual Differences Perspective on Coping and Emotional Regulation." *Perspectives on Psychological Science* 8(6) (2013):591-612. https://doi.org/10.1177/1745691613504116.

12. Thomas L. Webb, Eleanor Miles, and Paschal Sheerhan, "Dealing with Feeling: A Meta-analysis of the Effectiveness of Strategies Derived from the Process Model of Emotion Regulation." *Psychological Bulletin* 138(4) (2012): 775-808. https://doi.org/10.1037/a0027600.

13. James J. Gross, "Emotion Regulation: Current Status and Future Prospects." *Psychological Inquiry* 26(1) (2015): 1-26. https://doi.org/10.1080/1047840X.2014.940781.

14. A. Zaccaro et al., "How Breath Control Can Change Your Life: A systematic review on Psycho-Physiological Correlates of Slow-Breathing." *Frontiers in Human Neuroscience* 12 (2018). https://doi.org/10.3389/fnhum.2018.00353.

15. Lisa Feldman-Barrett, *How Emotions Are Made: The Secret Life of the Brain* (New York: Pan Macmillan, 2017).

16. Michelle G. Craske, Michael Treanor, Chris Conway, Tomislav Zbozinek, and Bram Vervliet, "Maximizing Exposure Therapy: An Inhibitory Learning Approach." *Behaviour Research and Therapy* 58, (2014): 10-23. https://doi.org/10.1016/j.brat.2014.04.006.

PRINCIPLE #5:

Resilience

I've missed more than 9,000 shots in my career. I've lost almost 300 games. Twenty-six times, I've been trusted to take the game-winning shot and missed. I've failed over and over and over again in my life. And that is why I succeed.

— *Michael Jordan*

How often do you think about winning averages? The all-time great baseball players are successful around 30 percent of the time they step up to bat. The most accurate of basketball players make a little over 33 percent of their shots. Gymnasts are scored based on how many points they lose from a perfect score, not how many points they earn, based on mistakes they make.

Beyond sports, consider how many other types of performances are no different. How many times does a top-producing salesperson get a "no" in proportion to a "yes"? Lawyers will lose trials, doctors will misdiagnose symptoms, and CEOs will make the wrong decisions about implementing strategies in response to volatile markets.

The wonderful thing about adversity is that it hones resilience, and resilience is a key factor in elite performance.

Adversity comes in many forms. There are things we cannot prepare for, such as last-minute changes and other circumstances that are beyond our control. These elements are inherent in high performance and are what make all performances odd-based events. Regardless of how much we prepare or how optimized we are, it's inevitable that we'll be confronted with something that we must respond to effectively to be our best when it matters most. Resilience allows us to return to top form after being challenged.

As suggested in the epigraph of this chapter, the best athletes learn to appreciate the opportunity to respond to adversity, and then leverage those opportunities to shape their success over the long-term. For all the game-winning shots Michael Jordan has missed, he's remembered most for the shots that he's made with the game on the line. Like Jordan, exceptional performers that learn to manage the adversity they encounter in their performance are more likely to be remembered for what they've done well. Effectively managing adversity keeps us on track to deliver our best performances rather than get derailed by the unexpected. As a result, the overall performance is of a higher quality and performers are seen as more masterful.

TONY HAWK: MAKING THE 900

The 1999 X Games ended with one of the greatest achievements in skateboarding history. Tony Hawk, at that time already considered one of the greatest skateboarders of all time, reached the peak of his career with the completion of two-and-a-half rotations in the air before momentarily landing on his feet and then collapsing into the arms of competitors with joy. It took nearly ten years of practice, failure, and resilience to get to that one moment, including multiple failures in the minutes before.

Tony Hawk had been trying to land a 900 (called the 900 for the degrees of rotation in two-and-a-half spins) for the last ten years. His pursuit of the 900 began in 1985, when Hawk hit a 720 (two full rotations) in a competition. Hawk became the first skateboarder ever to land such a trick, and in his quest for all-time greatness, he continued to push the envelope. Like other top performers, once Hawk reached the pinnacle, it was simply time to find another mountain to climb.

Three years later, Hawk attempted his first 900. It did not go well. Over a decade of practicing the 900 left him with a litany of injuries: concussions, cracked ribs, lost teeth, and back problems resulted as a byproduct of missed attempts. In reply to questions about his failed attempts, he said, "Some tricks you think you will never get. All you can do is keep at it." A decade of persistence and resilience positioned Hawk for one of the pinnacle moments in action sports history.

In interviews after the event, we can hear how resilient he was in the moments leading up to the successful 900. His competitors (who turned into collaborators and social support during the successful jump) remarked that Tony seemed to only have two possible outcomes on the table that night: hitting the 900 or "killing himself trying."

Although it didn't quite look like Tony was going to kill himself trying, the night was not initially very kind to Tony. Leading up to his first attempted 900, Tony reported that he had hit two tricks that, in his mind, were harder. He noticed that he had time left in the competition, and someone told him that the event announcer had asked the crowd if they wanted to see a 900.

What happened next is a quintessential lesson in resilience. On his first few attempts, Tony rose up into the air and began to spin, only to have his board fly out from underneath him, leaving him on his knees. In reflecting on those moments, Tony said, "I started to feel like this could be the ultimate disappointment, you know, if I just can't do it." The internal shift that happened next inside Tony's thinking sparked the resilience. "So, that's why I was willing to just stick in it, if possible. If it meant that I was going to get taken out, or taken to the hospital, so be it. It'll be worth the effort." He had shifted from the threat of the event, the ultimate disappointment, to the challenge, and in the challenge finding the drive to attempt the trick.

That mental shift alone didn't produce the results Tony was looking for. He also benefited from a group of competitors-turned-friends and a crowd that seemed to instinctively appreciate the value of social support in facilitating elite performance. In a tremendous display of competitive humility, four other all-time great skateboarders put their own goals aside to support Tony, with the announcer and the crowd offering words of encouragement after each attempt.

Tony also recognized how his built environment was facilitating some resilient responding. In an interview after the event, he remarked how his spinning in the trick was more consistent than it had been in the past, because the ramp he was competing on was sturdier than others he had used. This consistency in his spin reinforced for Hawk that completing the trick was possible. What was happening was that Hawk's sense of self-efficacy was increasing. During the next few attempts, Tony focused on the adjustments he needed to make to get closer to his goal. Slight shifts in his weight and body position were the difference between ending up on his back or his knees or standing straight up. This is self-regulated learning and the development of expertise in action.

On the eleventh attempt, after an unparalleled display of staying focused and optimizing his own energy, Hawk dropped into the ramp, used two simple jumps to gain speed and momentum, and, on his third trip up the ramp, launched into a complete two-and-a-half spin cycle, landing on his feet and barely grazing the bottom of the ramp with his hand. In an epic display of resilience, Tony Hawk completed the 900.

After conquering the 900, Tony Hawk retired from professional skateboarding, though he continued to skateboard recreationally. In reflecting on his achievement, he remarked to *People* magazine in 2019 that he "didn't expect it to be such a struggle as it was, and so at that moment, I very much felt like that's the last one I want to do." Yet, with a bit of time and psychological distance (something we'll cover a bit later as a resilience tool), he laughed and said, "But, you know, now that I'm a little bit further away from that moment, who knows?"

RESILIENCE IN ACTION

The definition of resilience that has made its way into our collective consciousness has centered on "bouncing back" in response to a perceived failure or adversity. The downside of that framing is an emphasis on resilience as something that either happens or doesn't, rather than a continuum of possible responses to adversity. This narrow definition of resilience comes from the Latin word *resilire*, which means to "jump back." The term was used to describe materials (not people) that returned to original form after pressure had been applied to alter them.

More recently, performance psychologists have started to define resilience in terms of an individual performer's ability to withstand pressure in order to maintain functioning and optimize performance.[1] As the science of resilience in psychology has advanced, necessarily so has the research expanded to take into consideration contextual and environmental factors that influence an individual's capacity to respond with resilience. What we know now is that resilience is a continuum influenced by a combination of factors within a person–environment context.[2]

This capacity to respond is critical to reaching full potential. In their comprehensive study of the experiences and traits of elite performers, Dave Collins and Áine MacNamara described a "rocky road" that elite performers must trace to the top, even going so far as to say that "talent needs trauma." The key message embedded in this work is that, for any of us to reach our full potential, we need to experience challenges and stressors that allow us to practice resilience skills, adapt, and ultimately facilitate enhanced performance in the future.[3]

We need some experience with adversity to learn how to respond resiliently. It's a bit like training a muscle. First, you stress the muscle with a new exercise. Then, you follow it with rest. Each new stressor increases adaptive capacity, which allows you to take on progressively harder challenges. In the case of our mind, overcoming stressors and practicing our coping gives us confidence in what we can handle the next time around. Resilience can even be detected at a biological level by tracking changes in our cells.[4] The key is to learn to seek growth, even when conditions don't support it.[5]

Modern psychological research on peak performers also provides us with direction on how we can increase our resilience in the moment. This research also supports the benefits of training our resilience: we experience our life more positively, achieve our goals more often, are more productive, and are rated more favorably by observers.[6] In fact, Diane Coutu, journalist and psychology editor at *Harvard Business Review*, noted that, "more than education, more than experience, a person's level of resilience will determine who succeeds and who fails. That's true in the cancer ward, it's true in the Olympics, and it's true in the boardroom."[7]

Resilience science suggests we can focus on two aspects of our performances to respond resiliently: proactive factors and reactive factors, each of which can be applied across all three phases of performance—before, during, and after the event. These factors can also be cultivated at the individual or environmental level. Collectively, proactive and reactive factors allow you to adequately prepare and cope with adversity and to maintain or even improve your level of performance in response to additional stress and pressure.

Over time, though, it's not enough to just build our own resources of resilience. The environment must be changed. Just changing what we think or how we cope with adversity won't last because so much of our behavior and experience is shaped by the environment we are in.

Consider, for a moment, your experience driving to a job you love versus a job you loathed (or at least didn't like so much). Chances are, as soon as you made the conscious decision to head to work, you noticed some changes in your mood or energy. Because your mind is anticipating the experience of the environment, it's proactively preparing you to respond to what you expect. Your need for resilience is being altered before you even show up.

Your experience will also be impacted by the social environment at your place of work. Even if you hold down a tough job, having close friends makes it more likely that you'll enjoy your work and stick around longer. Conversely, even if you enjoy your job, low social support is a recipe for an early exit. The social circumstances, in effect, *are* our environment. No matter how much you train your individual ability to cope with these circumstances, the social nature of our existence is likely to eventually overwhelm you, and you'll either leave or underperform. Resilience is a person–environment interaction.

Now for the good news: we can train resilience. And, resilience training has positive effects on both individual well-being and performance. By practicing the resilience skills we will cover in the next section, any individual can tap into the so-called "ordinary magic" of responding to adversity.[8] These same skills can also enhance peak performance.

The Mental Makeup of Resilient Responders

The most important factors for resilience in high performers are (1) a positive and proactive personality, (2) experience and learning, (3) a sense of control, (4) the ability to adapt positively to change and respond creatively to novelty, and (5) balance and perspective.[9] This includes things like confidence in our ability to succeed, understanding our motivation, keeping the bigger picture in mind when adversity strikes, and maintaining a sense of hope as pressure or adversity ebbs and flows. What these characteristics allow for is a repertoire of responses to a range of adversities that might come our way.

What does it mean to have a positive and proactive personality? It means we are open to experiences (growth oriented and challenge seeking), dutiful in our approach to work, and conscientious, optimistic, and realistic.[10] These characteristics allow high performers to make sense of adverse experiences or pressure-filled events in an adaptive way. They see the experience as an opportunity to be challenged and to grow rather than perceive experience as a threat to their ego (more on this later). It's from this positive posture toward adversity or pressure that the rest of the internal resilience characteristics can flow. Without being open to an experience, methodical in approach, and challenge seeking and growth oriented, it would be hard to reap the benefits and cultivate the characteristics associated with resilience in performers.

As we explored above, we do need some reps to get resilient. Experience and learning teach us what works, what doesn't work, and how we can respond more effectively in the future. While I'd never willingly wish adversity on anyone, the adversity you experience is an opportunity for you to gain the experience you need to take on progressively higher, harder challenges. The more you face, the more you can learn. The more you learn, the better you'll be.

All this learning gives you a sense of control when adversity strikes in the future. Resilience is a skill. I'll emphasize again that practice that closely resembles the conditions of the performance itself is the best kind of practice we can get. It's no different for resilience, because all those adverse experiences give us a sense of what we can do and build our confidence in our execution in the future. When we're in control and in the driver's seat, it's also much easier to respond adaptively to changing circumstances.

Sometimes, though, there will be things we simply can't overcome right away. Like Tony Hawk, you may not nail the 900 on your first or even tenth attempt. In these cases, we need the ability to maintain a sense of balance and perspective that our failures are not fatal or final. We need to remember that there will be a chance to try again, and like Hawk, if we're willing to put in greater effort, we may just reap the rewards on the other side.

Environmental Factors and Resilience

Of the environmental factors most important for high performers to be resilient, social support is the most significant. Like in our example of driving to work, simply changing a performer's internal approach to adversity can help, but without a system or environment to sustain that change and support when necessary, it's challenging to sustain resilience over the long term. We need support from peers, coaches, and mentors who can help us develop our skills when we're falling short and offer support when we aren't sure if we should continue down a particular path. The best athletes in the world still have coaches, after all. Pressure and adversity test all of our mettle. Social support can be the boon we need to continue when failure strikes.

Resilience abounds in systems structured to promote adaptive, resilient responses. Performers who respond resiliently create a high-performance environment, made up mainly of supportive, challenging, and compassionate people around them. These people help maintain and enhance their energetic resources, offer guidance and suggestions, and provide the essentials necessary for performance.

For example, it's difficult enough to close a sale for even the best of salespeople. It's one of the toughest jobs out there. If this same salesperson has a boss who is overly critical and unsupportive, and continually presents stretch goals knowing those goals are far beyond the capability of the salesperson, even a person with the utmost proactive and positive personality will become defeated and deflated.

In contrast, a salesperson with even a moderately positive and proactive personality working with a boss who appropriately challenges them, provides them with the basic resources necessary to succeed and more, and facilitates a supportive environment amongst the sales team, is much more likely to respond resiliently to failure. An individual can cultivate the characteristics internally to help them be resilient when it matters most, but the curation of the social support system can help high performers take their resilience over the top. In fact, social support is one of the best predictors we have of resilience and quality of life.

Putting Resilience into Practice

The highest performers in the world need resilience to reach the peak. In a study of twelve Olympic champions who were surveyed about their sport experiences, each of them reported that the ability to withstand pressure and act resiliently was critical to their success. There is no such thing as a top performance that *doesn't* have some degree of adversity. Think back to the stories of Tom Brady, Tony Hawk, and Shawn Mendes. Some of the adversity is internal and some is external. But there's no such thing as smooth sailing to a championship. To separate the best from the rest, we need both the individual capacity to respond resiliently and resilient social support around us to facilitate peak performance.

The research on resilience in Olympians informs a range of what we can do as performers to enhance our own resilience. The two most critical skills for responding effectively to pressure and adversity are challenge appraisals and metacognition. The factors can also influence resilience in the moment, as the most resilient individuals will match the necessary psychological skill or factor to the environmental stressor.

Challenge Appraisals

The highest performers make sense of the pressure or adversity by seeing it as a challenge to overcome or an opportunity to demonstrate what they are capable of. People naturally frame stressful situations as either a challenge or a threat, and this framing has a downstream impact on our physiology and psychology as we begin to interact with the stressor.[11]

At the simplest level, we tend to think of pressure or a stressor as a challenge when we believe we have the resources to deal with it effectively, and a threat when we are concerned it might overwhelm us. This difference in framing is the difference between feeling anxious or energized, in control or spiraling, and ready or overwhelmed. And it's all within our control.

There are two aspects to appraisals: our primary response and our secondary response. Step 1 is about determining whether the pressure or adversity is impacting us in the pursuit of our goals and its implications. Step 2 is about determining whether we believe we have the resources to cope with the problem at hand.

We can train ourselves to make challenge appraisals more readily. It starts with the language we use when talking to ourselves. Self-talk is an important self-regulation strategy.[12] It allows us to actively influence the way we are processing a stressor or adversity. By either using *distanced* self-talk (referring to ourselves in the second or third person) or *motivating* self-talk (hyping ourselves up to believe we have the resources), we can proactively process pressure as a challenge to be overcome rather than a threat to our ego.

Coach's Corner: Four Appraisals that Turn Stress into a Superpower

In my work with the NBA, I've found that there are four research-supported appraisals we can use to turn stress into a superpower and make our appraisals work for, rather than against, us.

The first is to frame the stress as a sign you care. Put simply, nobody feels stress about something that isn't important to them. When you're under pressure or adversity strikes, you only experience a change in your physiology because it matters to you. Rather than seeing it as a sign that something is wrong, you can interpret stress as a signal that you're engaged in something important.

The second appraisal I teach players is to categorize their nervous state as "excitement" instead of "anxiety." In our culture, we've been socialized to believe that stress is "bad," but it's really just your brain and body preparing you to do something effortful. Cortisol isn't a stress hormone; it's an energy hormone. And all that energy is excitement about the opportunity before you!

The third way to appraise a stressor is to look at it as a necessary component of success—determination. Your brain is getting you ready to give more effort, so you can persist through this adversity and make progress on something that matters to you.

Finally, you can learn to see the adversity as enhancing. It's kind of like the idea that pressure creates diamonds. When adversity strikes and your mind starts to see it as a threat, you can remind yourself that this adversity is making you better. It's another rep to get, and another opportunity to show what you're made of. And, once you overcome it, you'll be even more confident in what you can do the next time.

Metacognition

To make any of these appraisals maximally effective, you've got to be able to notice your implicit assumptions and the natural appraisals you make. You have to engage in what psychologists call *metacognition*, or just "thinking about thinking." To appraise effectively, you have to think about your default and then think about the best framing to deploy here and now.

Regarding resilience, metacognition refers to becoming aware of the thoughts that we are thinking under pressure or in the face of adversity, and recognizing how those thoughts are influencing our responses and physiology. High performers evaluate these thoughts and then proactively steer them in a direction that facilitates performance. For example, an athlete who is up against a particularly good opponent might initially experience self-talk that is threat-oriented (along the lines of "that player won their last match and is really good") but change it to challenge-oriented self-talk (such as, "I'm ready to show what I can do against one of the best"). The switch the athlete makes aligns their thinking, energy, and physiology to help them better meet the demands of the performance at hand. But without awareness of negative self-talk, the athlete will be stuck in response mode, fighting not only a worthy opponent but their own self-limiting beliefs and impacted physiology.

Metacognition is a skill we can develop through some practices we've already learned, too. Mindfulness meditation improves our ability to detect unhelpful thinking, and to let it go and redirect it appropriately. The more you practice, the better able you'll be to detect subtle thought patterns that undermine your performance and reposition them as something more helpful.

One of the main ways we learn to think about our thinking and to appraise effectively is through the feedback of people around us. The people in our environment actively shape our mindset by the language they use. They can activate metacognition if they say something that stands in stark contrast to what we believe, such as when someone gives you a compliment and it takes you a moment to process it, because it doesn't fit with the internal narrative you have for yourself. People around us can also activate our appraisals. If you've ever been around someone who's negative all the time, you've probably noticed how it drains your energy. They're subconsciously (and probably unintentionally, I hope) changing the way your mind is framing your experience.

For that reason, resilient performers have to work hard to surround themselves with the right people. Those people come with us, everywhere we go, in the form of our self-talk and internal experience.

More Resilience Factors

Social Support

No elite athlete reaches the peak alone. The best athletes in the world have coaches, athletic trainers, strength and conditioning coaches, nutritionists, and more available to them, each with a focus on helping the athlete be their best. Even in individual sport competitions, we can see the importance of these supporters when athletes are facing adversity. Note how the great tennis player will look for their coach in the stands when they are down a set, or the track athlete will listen for their coach's pacing and words of encouragement during a race to keep pushing. No elite performance happens in a vacuum; building a team of supporters is critical to being your best when it matters most. As Deontay Wilder said, "There's no 'I' in team, but there is an 'I' in the ring. That 'I' in the ring is nothing without the team that gets you there."

Social support helps at all stages of the performance continuum. Before a performance even occurs, having good social support raises our baseline ability to manage stress. This effect shows up at the physiological level: performers with good social support have lower heart rates, blood pressure, and cardiovascular responses to stress.[13] As we saw during Tony Hawk's attempts of the 900, having social support during performance can also allow us to maintain a facilitative response in the face of adversity. Social support can prevent threat appraisals[14] and can be a source of information to enhance performance when we're faced with a novel challenge. After our performance is done, social support can enhance effective recovery.[15] High performance needs a network.

This facilitation effect is a function of our evolution. In fact, people have evolved an incredible capacity to regulate each other's energy efficiency.[16] With a simple hug or words of affirmation, you can improve someone's performance. In fact, doing something nice for someone else restores your own energy efficiency.

Our social network also plays a big role in the next two factors we'll cover: motivation and confidence. It's quite common for professional athletes, founders, and elite military members to be doing what they do for someone else. In most Hall-of-Fame speeches, the best athletes first thank the people around them for driving them and giving them purpose, and for good reason. Other people keep us going and boost us up when we need it most.

Motivation

During pressure-packed moments or consistent confrontation with adversity, it's common for high performers to question themselves. If the pressure or adversity persists, performers may start to give up and retreat. This response is a milder version of what psychologists have termed "learned helplessness," or the idea that, at a certain point, exposure to something unpleasant (like stress or adversity) will lead people to actively try to avoid that unpleasant stimulus. In other words, under pressure and in the face of adversity, one normal, natural, and unhelpful human response is to try and walk away.

In these moments, resilient performers look to embrace the challenge. Motivation is critical to success. When the going gets tough, they either tap into their personal values, a sense of who they want to become by going through the adversity, or their social connections, the people who make the adversity worth it. The most resilient performers use their values and social networks to energize them.

One of the most meaningful lessons in motivation, persistence, and resilience comes from Austrian psychiatrist Viktor Frankl, author of *Man's Search for Meaning*. First published in 1946, Frankl detailed the horrendous experiences of surviving a Nazi death camp in World War II. Frankl revealed that what enabled him to want to continue living, day after day, was finding his true "meaning." This meaning, his "logos," was inspired both by the idea of reuniting with his wife and by sending a message to others in the camp about surviving. In the case of Frankl, both personal values and deep social connection served as critical sources of motivation that allowed him to persist through the most heinous of circumstances.

Since Frankl's work on meaning, psychologists have integrated a sense of higher purpose or deeper meaning into their work as a mechanism for enhancing motivation in the face of great adversity or pressure. For today's peak performer, this mechanism can be described by answering one question: Who do you want to become?

This question offers a tremendous, evergreen source of resilience. We can *always* be working on becoming the best version of ourselves, and when adversity strikes, it's just an opportunity to ask ourselves, "How would the person I want to be respond in this situation?" The act of viewing this idealized future version of ourselves can give us the energy we need to keep going when the going is tough.

Confidence

When we're confronted with pressure or adversity, to succeed, we need to believe that we have what it takes. This sense of confidence—or the degree of certainty we have about our ability to succeed in that moment—plays a big part in facilitating an appraisal of an event as a challenge or a threat. That appraisal is further facilitated by the people around us, and whether or not they believe in us. For many athletes I've worked with, no source of self-belief is greater than their coach believing in them. Having the confidence of our role models and leaders gives us the confidence we need to respond resiliently.

Confidence can come from other sources too. For a brief recap, remember that one of the main sources of confidence we have is our *past experience*. High performers reflect on past successes and recall how they received support from coaches and peers; how they meticulously prepared for an event and dealt with factors such as adversity and stress; and how they assessed their strengths and limitations. Confidence is the nemesis of adversity.

Coach's Corner: Focus as a Source of Resilience

One other source of resilience we can access is focus. Having the ability to shift our focus is about ensuring that we stay locked in on aspects of performance that will help us perform at our best, for example by maintaining our attention on our play, rather than shifting our attention to some aspect of adversity or pressure and how this might affect the outcome of our performance. Focusing on the outcomes of performance tends to increase anxiety and reduce our sense of control, both of which are likely to negatively impact our performance under pressure.

The best performers use their focus to actively let go of pressure or adversity once the moment has passed. A famous sport psychologist in baseball, Ken Ravizza, used to symbolically ask his athletes to "flush" mistakes down a small toilet in their dugout. The symbolism worked by allowing athletes to attend to the mistake, and then shift their focus back to performance.

Adversity is a quintessential element of performance. No pitch goes perfectly, no game is without its successes and failures, no parent will get it right 100 percent of the time. It's not about getting it perfect. It's about meeting adversity, building your resilience skills to become stronger over time, and confidently meeting ever-more-difficult challenges.

ZOSIA TEACHES US A VALUABLE LESSON

There's no better illustration of resilience than a young child. My daughter, Zosia, recently turned one and a half and, as any parent of a toddler is familiar with, has become a walking accident. She seems to fall over at least once a minute. And yet, each time, she smiles, gets up, and tries again.

Nowhere was this more evident than during a recent trip to the park. She stumbled up to some stairs and slowly, methodically, tried to lift herself up, one by one. There were only five stairs, but each step was met with a swift fall to the ground.

As a parent, it's incredibly challenging to watch your kid fall repeatedly. You want to jump in, rescue them, and help them avoid injury. You wish you could just will them to mastery right away. And yet, the most important lessons are in the falling down and getting up.

In fact, most adults I know would stop trying after falling five-plus times going up and down the stairs. But kids don't. They have a natural resilience, because they're motivated to learn and grow. We all are, but it gets stymied as we get older so that we don't "embarrass" ourselves. Kids don't have this problem—they're motivated to learn, confident they can do it, focused on a goal, supported by parents, and get an awful lot of practice.

The same things that allowed my daughter to master the staircase can help any performer master their own challenges. Resilience isn't about not messing up, but rather about making the most of mistakes you make. So, the next time you are faced with a challenge, try asking yourself what a toddler would do (tantrums excluded). You'll be amazed at the results.

* * *

Preparation, Immersion, Adaptability, Optimizing Energy, and Resilience. As you go forward in your quest to lift your performance, keep a journal or diary of how these skills and traits are playing out. If a game or business presentation doesn't go as well as you had planned, reflect on why. Why did performance gaps show up and what steps will you take to correct them? Use the Coach's Corner tips to guide you. Take cues from the stories and examples to do better next time. Success is about trying and trying again.

Continue to reflect, act, and take notes. No matter where your call to greatness comes from, remember you can influence the odds in your favor. Good luck.

ENDNOTES

1. Mustafa Sarkar and David Fletcher, "Ordinary Magic, Extraordinary Performance: Psychological Resilience and Thriving in High Achievers." *Sport, Exercise, and Performance Psychology* 3(1): 46. https://doi.org/10.1037/spy0000003.

2. Sarkar and Fletcher, "Ordinary Magic."

3. Dave Collins and Aine MacNamara, "The Rocky Road to the Top: Why Talent Needs Trauma." *Sports Medicine* 42(11) (2012): 907-914.

4. Michael J. Reed, Benjamin E. Wolfe, and L. Michael Romero, "Is Resilience a Unifying Concept for the Biological Sciences?" *iScience* 27(5) (2024). https://doi.org/10.10116/j.sci2024.109478.

5. Sheldon, *Freely Determined*.

6. Mustafa Sarkar and David Fletcher, "How Resilience Training Can Enhance Wellbeing and Performance." In M. F. Crane (Ed.), *Managing for Resilience: A Practical Guide for Employee Wellbeing and Organizational Performance* (London: Routledge/Taylor & Francis Group, 2017): 227-237.

7. Diane Coutu, "How Resilience Works." *Harvard Business Review* (May 2002).

8. Ann S. Masten, "Ordinary Magic: Resilience Processes in Development." *American Psychologist* 56(3) (2001): 227. https://doi.org/10.1037/0003-066X.56.3.227.

9. Sarkar and Fletcher, "Resilience Training."

10. Ibid.

11. Collins and MacNamara, "The Rocky Road to the Top." Joe Tomaka, Jim Blascovich, Robert M. Kelsey, and Christopher L. Leitten, "Subjective, Physiological, and Behavioral Effects of Threat and Challenge Appraisal." *Journal of Personality and Social Psychology* 65(2) (1993): 248.

12. Sarkar and Fletcher, "Resilience Training."

13. Coutu, "How Resilience Works."

14. Masten, "Ordinary Magic."

15. Tomaka, "Subjective, Physiological, and Behavioral Effects of Threat and Challenge Appraisal."

16. Ethan Kross et al., "Self-Talk as a Regulatory Mechanism: How You Do It Matters." *Journal of Personality and Social Psychology* 106(2) (2014): 304-324. https://doi.org/10.1037/a0035173.

CONCLUSION:
WE ARE ALL CALLED TO GREATNESS

I wrote this book because I believe everybody is a performer. We all have something that we want to be great at doing. In fact, I believe the drive to be great is one of the most powerful and universal experiences. I've never met anyone who doesn't want to push themselves forward in a domain they care about a lot.

Yet despite that natural human desire, these skills and principles don't show up anywhere in a school curriculum. Most of them are left out of sports training until well into an athlete's career. This is a big problem. Too many aspiring athletes underperform for far too long, and not because they want to, but because they've never been taught how to do it right.

The skills and principles laid out in this book, when applied, can right that wrong. They are the foundation to my approach to coaching performance. I believe they can help anyone perform at their best when it matters most. When we watch athletes perform at the top of their game, we often think of them as superhuman. Fortunately, how they train mentally, emotionally, and physically leaves important clues for us all about how we too can become superhuman in our own way in our own performance.

Throughout this book, we've covered some core psychological skills that can help you be more consistent, committed, and confident in the work you do. You've learned to frame your stressors appropriately, how to be more present, what you can do when adversity strikes, and how to set yourself up for long-term success. You've also learned how to progressively increase what you're capable of doing and how to prepare so that no performance, from parenting to pitching investors, is too big.

In Part 1, we talked about the qualities of typical performance. You learned about adaptive capacity and how to increase what's possible for you. We explored mental strength and how to build your confidence. You learned about psychological flexibility, which can help you to stay both physically and mentally healthy. And you learned about the single skill that separates the best from the rest—self-regulation—and what you can do to develop it.

From there we transitioned to peak performance, discussed in Part 2. You learned about quality preparation (which rarely gets covered in mindset books), how to respond resiliently and stay adaptive, and what's needed to manage your energy. You were introduced to several strategies you can use to help yourself think, feel, and perform better.

Armed with the tools and techniques you've discovered, you're now better positioned to help yourself and those around you to reach their full potential. You and everyone you know have the chance to be great. You just have to answer the call.

ACKNOWLEDGMENTS

More people deserve credit for helping this work become a reality than I can reasonably mention or remember. I'm going to do my best anyway.

First, my parents. I grew up genuinely believing there was nothing I couldn't do. Their enthusiasm to take on any challenge that comes along has always given me confidence. Writing a book tested the limits of my endurance. I love you. Thank you for believing in me.

In sport psychology: Scott Goldman, Amy Athey, and Trent Petrie. Each of you has been instrumental in my development and professional path. It's doubtful anyone would care what I had to say if you hadn't helped me avoid so many mistakes.

Then there's my brother-in-law, Tyler, who gave the first draft of this thing a read from front to back and encouraged me to keep going, albeit with a healthy dose of suggested edits. I might have given up on publishing if you hadn't told me my first draft wasn't a complete dumpster fire. Thanks for making sure I finished.

I wouldn't have gotten to a draft of anything if it wasn't for Cody Royle, who's been consistently pushing me to share what I think with the world, giving me feedback on my writing, and answering the call when I feel like I have nothing to say.

INDEX

Abbott, Jim, 167–68, 169
Abdul-Jabbar, Kareem, 143
acceptance, 84–85, 180, 181
adaptation, 18, 61, 92, 163, 165–83
adaptive capacity, 3–23, 212
adversity, 60–61, 204, 208, 211–23
anxiety, 140, 186–87, 196, 218, 223
 reducing, 21, 82, 131–33, 198–99
arousal, 11, 132–33, 186–88, 190, 192, 199, 201, 203
 Yerkes-Dodson Law, 131–32, 194
attentional deployment, 199–200
automaticity, 120, 127, 128–29
autonomy, 63, 66
avoidance, 63, 89–92
awareness, 33, 70–71, 144, 147–48, 171–72, 219. *See also* self-awareness

Bandura, Albert, 31
Beckham Jr., Odell, 176–77
Belichick, Bill, 11, 39, 93–94
Beyonce, 188
Biles, Simone, 4, 82
Brady, Tom, 11, 34, 54, 73–75, 98, 127, 146–47, 216
breathing, 88, 137–38, 156, 180, 199
Bryant, Kobe, 99, 188, 193–94

capacity. *See* adaptive capacity
challenge appraisals, 217–18
challenge mindset, 60, 62–63, 191
coaches, 10, 17, 81, 93–94, 220
Coach's Corner
 The Confidence Résumé, 31–32
 Focus as a Source of Resilience, 223
 Four Appraisals that Turn Stress into a Superpower, 218
 Identifying Values, 174–75
 Leaves on a Stream, 88
 Providing Effective Feedback, 126
 Readiness and Regulation, 101
 The Role of Feedback in Self-Awareness, 17
 Short-Term Strategies to Perform in the Moment, 197
 Sporting Genius, 35–36
 Tips on Leveraging External Focus, 151
 Tips to Improve Quality of Sleep, 8
cognitive fusion, 156
Collins, Dave, 212
committed action, 176–77
commitment, 42–43, 144–45, 153–54, 159–61, 173
Common Core State Standards, 13–14
competition plans, 133, 141

confidence, 30–34, 35–36, 37, 40–42, 100, 222–23. *See also* self-belief; self-efficacy
    building confidence, 128–33
context sensitivity, 101–3
control, 61, 66. *See also* self-control
    controlling the controllables, 99–104, 133–35, 138–39
cortisol, 11, 102, 218
Coutu, Diane, 212
Crum, Dr. Alia, 12, 62–63
Curry, Steph, 122

Deci, Edward, 65–66
deconstruction, 196
defusion, 83, 170, 177–80
deliberate practice, 120, 124–27, 139
Donald, Aaron, 33
Duckworth, Angela, 55

elite performance, 169–74
emotion. *See* feelings
endurance, 53–76
energy efficiency, 10, 187, 190–97, 201–2, 221
energy optimization, 185–204
engagement, 173–74
Ericsson, Anders, 124–25
eudaimonia, 69–70
Eurich, Dr. Tasha, 15, 18–20
executives, 9, 31, 40–42, 86, 175
exercise, 21–22, 57–58
experience
    learning from, 61
    mastery experiences, 31, 32, 129

fear
    managing, 118–119, 195
    overcoming, 28–30, 201

Feared Stimulus Tactic, 201
Federer, Roger, 27, 34, 35, 38–39, 48–49, 97, 99
feedback, 10, 16, 17, 18–19, 40–42, 61, 94, 103–4, 125–26, 219–20
feelings, 84–85, 91, 192, 193
flexibility. *See* psychological flexibility
flow, 101, 113, 124, 126, 154
focus, 148–53, 157–58, 181, 223
framing, 11–13, 139–40, 217. *See also* reframing
Frankl, Victor, 222
Franklin, Benjamin, 89
Free Solo, 33, 116

Gandhi, Mahatma, 3
goals, 36–39, 137, 159–60, 176–177
Goldilocks principle, 72, 190–91
Google, 9
Gray, Wayne D., 80
grit, 55–57, 154

Hamilton, Lewis, 4, 22–23
Hawk, Tony, 209–11
hedonic treadmill, 68–69
Higgins, Joe, 35–36
Hill, Bob, 145
Honnold, Alex, 28–29, 33–34, 115, 116–19, 123, 201
hydration, 8

identifying obstacles, 160–61
immersion, 143–63
Individual Zone of Optimal Functioning (IZOF), 131–32, 141, 190–91, 203
inner drive, 45–48

James, LeBron, 54
Jenkins, Sally, 47

Jeter, Derek, 53
Jha, Dr. Amisha, 155
Jobs, Steve, 43
Johari Window, 18–20
Johnson, Shawn, 185
Jordan, Michael, 11, 54, 98, 107, 207, 208
journaling, 20, 158–59, 179–80, 224–25

Kashdan, Todd, 81–82
Kipchoge, Eliud, 79
Kotler, Steven, 55–56
Kross, Ethan, 130

labeling, 179
Lindstedt, John K., 80
Love, Kevin, 4

MacNamara, Áine, 212
marshmallow test, 43–45
meaning and purpose, 67–73
Mendes, Shawn, 186–88, 191, 198, 216
mental contrasting and implementation intentions, 136–37, 141, 159
mental health, 4–5, 10, 59, 69, 81, 94
mental strength, 23, 27–50
Messi, Leo, 54, 152–53
metacognition, 218–220
mindfulness, 87, 181, 182
mindfulness meditation, 20, 154–58, 179, 219
Mischel, Walter, 43–44
Monkey Business Illusion, 149
monitoring, 158–59
monitoring progress, 36, 106,
motivation, 55, 64–67, 221–22
Motivation Intensity Theory, 64–65

New England Patriots, 73, 93–94, 146–47

No Child Left Behind, 13–14
nutrition, 8, 22

Olympic athletes, 35, 45–46, 47, 68–69, 189, 216
openness, 170–71
Osaka, Naomi, 4, 82

Parrish, Shane, 163, 166
passion, 55–57
Payton, Walter, 86–87, 144–145, 162–63
peak performance, 18–20, 80, 99, 113–14, 147, 157, 172, 192
performance anxiety, 131–33
perseverance, 57–58
perspective, 61–62
Phelps, Michael, 4, 47–48
physicians, 99, 134–35, 171, 202–3
physiology, 31–34, 99–104, 131–33, 137–38, 147, 188–95, 219
play, 13–14
positivity, 60–61
preparation, 116–41. *See also* psychological preparation
 deliberate practice, 120, 124–27, 139
 pre-performance routines, 132, 135–36
 purposeful practice, 120–24, 135–40
present moment focus, 181
proactivity, 60–61
process goals, 37, 137
Project Aristotle, 9
psychological flexibility, 76, 79–95, 168–74, 180
psychological preparation, 118, 128–35, 140
public speaking, 123–24, 134, 191
purpose and meaning, 67–73
purposeful practice, 120–24, 135–40

readiness, 101, 118–20, 139
reframing, 132–33, 187, 198–99
reflection, 175
regulation, 188, 190–95. *See also* self-regulation
repertoire of behaviors, 103, 214
representativeness, 123–24, 141
resilience, 10, 55, 58–64, 207–25
rote exercise, 121
Rottenberg, Jonathan, 81–82
Ryan, Richard, 65–66

Saban, Nick, 93–94
sales, 126, 134, 137–39, 199–200, 216
Sarkar, Mustafa, 60–62
self-as-context, 85, 172, 181
self-awareness, 15–21, 22, 154–55, 158
self-belief, 34–43
self-care, 6, 21–23
self-complexity, 85–87
self-confidence. *See* self-efficacy
self-control, 43–45, 98
self-determination, 63, 65–67
self-efficacy, 31–34, 129, 131, 222–23
self-regulation, 95, 97–108, 144, 217
self-talk, 32–34, 130, 131, 136, 178–79, 186, 188, 217, 219–20
semantic satiation, 178–79
Simons, Daniel J., 149
situation modification, 197–98
sleep, 6–8

SMART goals, 159–60, 176
Smith, Will, 165
social support, 9–11, 15–16, 62, 67, 210, 213, 215–16, 220–21
stress
    management, 11–12, 62–63, 220
    mindsets, 12–13, 218
sunlight, 21
surgeons. *See* physicians
Swift, Taylor, 173

Taurasi, Diana, 100–101
teamwork, 9–11, 12–13
threat mindset, 191
Toronto Raptors, 112

University of Alabama Crimson Tide, 93–94
US Army Rangers, 160–61
US Parajumpers, 181–82, 196–87

values, 15–17, 19, 56–57, 70–72, 80, 83, 84–85, 88–93, 169, 173, 174–77, 180, 221–22
variation in practice, 122
verbal persuasion. *See* self-talk

wellness foundations, 5–14
Wilder, Deontay, 220
Woods, Tiger, 42–43, 107–8

Yerkes-Dodson Law, 131–32, 194

ABOUT THE AUTHOR

Dr. Alex Auerbach is a counseling and performance psychologist who has coached athletes at the major league and Olympic ranks. Most recently, he served as the Senior Director of Wellness and Development for the Toronto Raptors. Dr. Auerbach has also worked with NCAA Division-I schools in the SEC, Pac-12, ACC, Big 12, and Conference USA. As an executive coach, he is in demand to build better leaders.

Dr. Auerbach earned his doctoral degree in counseling psychology with a specialization in sport and performance psychology from the University of North Texas. He has a master's degree in business administration from Salve Regina University and a bachelor's degree in business administration from the University of Arizona.

www.ingramcontent.com/pod-product-compliance
Lightning Source LLC
LaVergne TN
LVHW090851120125
801001LV00002B/96